The Sacred Cross

A Transformational
Spiritual Tool for Life

By Anastacia J. Nutt

Co-Founder, Facilitator
The Path of the Ceremonial Arts

The Sacred Cross: A Transformational Spiritual Tool for Life

By Anastacia J. Nutt

Published by:
R J Stewart Books
PO Box 802
Arcata CA 95518
www.rjstewart.net

Printed in the United States of America and in the United Kingdom

A Catalogue record for this book is available from the Library of Congress.

ISBN: 978-0-9819246-6-3

The Sacred Cross:

A Transformational Spiritual Tool for Life

Introduction

The Path of the Ceremonial Arts (PCA) is a three year community-based spiritual and ceremonial training program that my beloved Priestess partners Lila Sophia Tresemer, Katharine Roske and I co-founded in 1999. Ten years later, we employ seven facilitators, teach an average of sixty students annually, have amassed a pool of nearly one-hundred graduates and have started an international program in Palestine/Israel. Our mission is simply *Remember, Heal, Transform*. Through these principles, we assist men and women of spirit to remember the sacred, unite with their soul's knowing and heal their human/divine relationships through the transformative power of community ritual. Though we hold fast to living and co-creating in the moment in an organic appreciation of our own unfolding, our foundation is built upon the strength of five primary tools used throughout all three years of study. Through this book and companion CD, one of these five tools is making its debut beyond our temple chalice and into the world. This tool is called The Sacred Cross.

Through my fifteen year engagement in spiritual and magical teaching, I have come to believe that the truth of who we are is not revealed in some sudden moment of "enlightenment";

instead it is woven throughout the course of our lives. It is a tapestry, woven of and by our own design, uniting the threads of the soul, self, Heaven and Earth. If, as men and women of spirit, we endeavor to *live* and *become* minus any one of these four threads, our cloth will not possess the strength to stand the tests of time. For we must know ourselves as one who is both human and Divine, Earth-bound and Heavens-found before we can weave the tapestry of our own wholeness. Though an intellectual appreciation of this truth may be spoken to with conviction by many, the grace and splendor that blossoms within the "simply human" to "divinely human" transformation can only be known by those who dedicate themselves to the practice of this preaching. Through a clear and accessible approach, The Sacred Cross provides a practice that supports the transition from our "simple humanity" (e.g. knowing only of and focusing only upon the material elements of our life) to our "Divine humanity" (e.g. knowing of our material self in partnership with the trans-human Divine all around and within us). Similar to the reset button on an electrical appliance, The Sacred Cross recalibrates our personal awareness and orientation away from insular states of consciousness that entrap us and toward unifying states of consciousness that liberate us. Plainly put, The Sacred Cross lifts us up into a synergistic embrace that exalts the basis for our thinking, feeling and actions. This exaltation affects our spiritual and magical work, our family and relational life, our professional pursuits and even our sleep.

You might assume that a tool with so many different applications and benefits would have to be somewhat complex in its design. You will be relieved to know that the truth is quite the contrary. The Sacred Cross is as simple and straightforward as the illustration upon the cover of this book.

Looking again at that image, you will see five simple components: four arms and a central heart which serves as their meeting place. These five components, and all they connect us to, comprise the promise and potential of The Sacred Cross in its entirety.

We live in a day and age when people are seeking real and enduring spiritual tools that bridge the gap between their simply human and divinely human consciousness. Within the genre of spiritual and magical tools available to us in this regard, the offerings of The Sacred Cross are exceptional in three additional ways. First, although rooted within the Western Mystery Tradition, The Cross is not linked to the teachings or practices of any specific religion. From the beginning, it has been used successfully in mixed groups of different traditions and spiritual orientations. Second, when consistently practiced, the spiritual depth of The Cross stimulates a transformational process within the body consciousness of the user that can lead to real and abiding positive changes in the life. Finally, while received in the 21st century, you will soon discover that the esoteric underpinnings of The Sacred Cross stretch back to the mystery teachings of ancient times. In summary, The Sacred Cross is appropriate for persons of various orientations, religions, lifestyles and skill levels, capable of fostering real and enduring change, and well rooted within tried and true ancient streams of wisdom. What more could we ask for from a spiritual or magical tool?

I have been working with The Cross, in its evolutionary forms, since 2002. My seven year engagement with this tool has allowed me to gradually and progressively build an experienced-based appreciation of all The Sacred Cross is and offers. In writing this book, I am grateful to have the opportunity to bring the power and promise of this wonderful tool to a wider audience of men and woman of spirit living and working beyond the chalice of PCA. Through this book, the fruits of my discovery will be offered in four parts. In *Part 1: The Foundations of The Sacred Cross*, we will explore the geometrical and historical origins of this tool. In *Part 2: Elements of The Sacred Cross*, our attentions will turn toward an explanation of each of the five components that comprise The Sacred Cross. In *Part 3: Practical Applications* we bring the components together to invoke The Cross using various methods; we will also learn the occasions for their use. Finally, our exploration will conclude with a discussion of the deeper applications and long-term benefits of using The Sacred Cross in *Part 4: The Esoteric Aspects of The Sacred Cross*.

Please note a companion CD set by the same name is also available to assist you with the meditations offered throughout this book. Though not required for this work, many find the CDs to be a helpful initial means of focusing their meditation practice with The Sacred Cross.

With these introductory elements in place, let us begin our discovery of The Sacred Cross in earnest.

Part 1: Foundations of The Sacred Cross

As mentioned in the Introduction, the physical structure of The Sacred Cross has five components: four arms and their confluence point in the center. In actuality, the four arms of The Sacred Cross compose what is known as an equal armed cross. Because it is so important to the foundation of our work, let's take a moment to explore the equal armed cross and the discipline that recognizes its unique qualities: Sacred Geometry.

> "Certain geometrical shapes have the power to reach deep into the unconscious and effect subtle changes in the mood of the observer. The property is perhaps most apparent when applied by a skillful architect. For example, visitors to classic Greek sites often experience a sense of inner tranquility that can linger for days or even weeks.[1]"

As you may have learned or observed, many of the forms found within the natural world possess certain mathematically precise design elements. For example, we see a pentagonal form when we slice an apple horizontally and the Fibonacci sequence in the arrangement of the seeds in a sunflower, the spiral of a sea shell or the curling of an ocean wave. Sacred Geometry is the art and discipline that explores the properties inherent within these naturally occurring and man-made geometric forms. Through its

---

[1] Fontana, David. The Secret Language of Symbols: A Visual Key to Symbols and Their Meanings, Chronicle Books, San Francisco, 1994., p 54.

application humans have discovered that the design of a tree, the human body, insect wings, music, shells, flowers and many other things possess mathematical harmonies and relationships. Further, these harmonies and relationships served as the foundation for architectural design in the ancient civilizations of Egypt, Cambodia, Peru, Greece and India. We know, from the study of their temples, homes, burial chambers and cities that by and large, these ancients endeavored to capture the magic inherent within the design of the natural world. In doing so, they did not intend to simply mimic the mathematical relationships found within the natural world. They endeavored to provide an everlasting connection between themselves and the Divine Creator. To fully appreciate the discipline known to us today as Sacred Geometry, we must realize that it is not used as a means to honor or show reverence for the creative design of the natural world; it is a means of creating a direct connection with, and thus experience of, the "consciousness" of the Divine Creator. Humans who lived within the societies that honored the principles of Sacred Geometry were able to discover the deeper truths veiled within these geometrical forms. They did so by being physically within or meditating upon particular sacred geometrical forms and expressions. In this way, they put themselves in direct connection to the spiritual power that dwells behind and moves through the forms. They knew that this connection possesses the potential to bring about changes in consciousness that foster exalted states of awareness. In modern times we have forgotten this way of working with the majesty of the natural world, choosing instead to believe that sacred images, forms and iconography "stand for" something. Please note, in our work with The Sacred Cross, we rely upon to the ancients' way of knowing and understanding. Thus when we work with The Sacred Cross or any other tool based upon Sacred

Geometry, nothing we do should be interpreted to "stand for" something else. Instead, we intend to place ourselves in a direct relationship with the forces infused within the form. Further, these forces possess the power to change our whole body consciousness. Given this, what is mediated through the geometrical form known as the equal armed cross?

The Roots of the Equal Armed Cross

The equal armed cross, also commonly referred to as the square cross, balanced cross, peaceful cross and Greek Cross, is found in the artwork and architecture of several ancient cultures. These cultures predate those that served as the seedbeds of Christianity, for whom the cross has become an enduring symbol. As we begin our study of the equal armed cross, the historical distinction between the roots of the cross and its application in "modern" Christianity is important. In fact, it was the fish and not the cross that was the initial Christian symbol in the first three centuries of the Christian era.[2]

When exploring the roots of the ancients' use of the equal armed cross, we are inevitably led back to the erection of sacred marker stones. There is evidence that sacred marker stones were found in ancient China, India, Mesopotamia and Mesoamerica. In the west, pre-European pagan cultures also erected tall, vertical slabs of stone in important or conspicuous places; we currently refer to these pre-European stone monuments as "market crosses." It is commonly understood that these forms embodied

---

[2] Bryce, Derek. Symbolism of the Celtic Cross, LLanerch Enterprises, Dyfed Wales, 1989.

the Axis Mundi, Tree of Life or world axis and thus expressed the union of Heaven and Earth[3].

Often market crosses stood in the center of an intersection or crossroads, where the "ways" came together. In the ancient world, these "conjunctions of the ways" were where oaths were taken, justice dispensed, important business conducted and proclamations spoken outward. Of considerable significance is the historical fact that these places were given the status of sanctuary where no person could be taken, attacked or harmed. In later centuries, the sacred function of providing sanctuary was co-opted by the Christian churches. There was no distinction between the sacred and secular life; the whole of the life was part of the sacred[4]. And in these instances, the stone marked the cross on the ground where two, three or four simple trackways came together. It was believed and experienced that in these places of conjunction, balance, harmony and unity naturally occurred and thus blessed all that transpired there.

In his web-based text, *Sun Disc to Crucifix The Cross*, Ian McNeil Cooke offers us a further glimpse into the pre-European past where additional examples of the equal armed cross are found.

> "The simple equal-armed cross is one of the nine primary geometric forms (i.e. those forms which combine to create all other shapes) found in nearly 400 examples of Irish megalithic rock-art so far discovered, all of which are associated with astronomically orientated passage mounds some 5-6000 years old. The cross is the third most common primary, being used in 34% of all known designs,

---

[3] Ibid.
[4] Bryce, Derek. Symbolism of the Celtic Cross, LLanerch Enterprises, Dyfed Wales, 1989.

and is usually combined with the circle - the commonest
primary - to make apparent solar, lunar or stellar symbols
which seem to refer specifically to the four or eight major
directions.

Crosses are also found on Neolithic pottery, usually
marked on the base, and it has been suggested that the four
arms of the cross, which can evolve into 4 or 8-armed
'turning' swastikas, represent the four phases of the moon
- waxing, full, waning and dark. What exactly was their
significance we shall probably never know but, what does
seem certain, is that the cross was one of many abstract
symbols having some religious meaning."

At this point we have a sense of the practical uses of the form
known as the equal armed cross in ancient cultures. This is
where I feel it is best to center our understanding of the roots of
this form. When researching any enduring symbol we are often
bombarded by many unsubstantiated claims and strange
findings. The equal armed cross is no exception. Popular
literature offers a plethora of "deep and ancient" traditional
meanings associated with the equal armed cross. However most
of these dissertations offer no references and seem only to be
made of the stuff that loosely supports the personal spiritual
agenda of the author.

It is in the word "conjunction" we find the key, for this
expresses the deepest roots of the form known as the equal
armed cross: the conjunction of four ways into a commonly fed
and shared center point. Given their expression, and the co-
opting of that expression in later spiritual and religious
traditions, it is the simplicity of "conjunction" that is expanded
and augmented in the other forms of the cross.

"Like the Tree of Life, the cross stands for the 'world
axis'...The cross, consequently, affirms the primary

relationship between the two worlds of the celestial and the earthly. But, in addition, because of the cross-piece which cuts cleanly across the upright, it stands for the conjunction of opposites, wedding the spiritual (or vertical) principle with the principle of the world of phenomena (or horizontal).[5]"

The Harmony of Four

A conjunction is a concurrent joining, merging or mingling of different things or energies. An equal armed cross embodies a conjunction in a very particular way. As a mingling or joining of four lines or arms, the equal armed cross opens the portals of our consciousness to the dynamic principle known as the "harmony of four." The harmony of four is a phrase used to describe the balanced power created by the coming together of four complementary elements or aspects. And as you know, there are many such aspects found within the natural world; examples include the four winds, the four seasons, the four stages of a life, the four bodily humors and the four elements. The basis of each of these various expressions is the number four. As we deepen our appreciation of the synergy inherent within the harmony of four, let's consider the potential and power of the "four" itself.

We see and experience the number four in several ways in the world of form: the legs of a table, the arms and legs of a human being, life stages, the number wheels on a car, the four-legged creatures and the external walls of our homes. What do these expressions of four sides, four legs, four angles, four posts, four walls tell us about the spiritual power that resides behind

---

[5] Cirlot, J. E. A Dictionary of Symbols, 2nd Edition, Dorset Press, New York, 1971, p. 70.

the number four itself? In each of these instances the number four offers a certain measure of stability. Our car driving on four wheels is more stable than the popular three-wheeled off road vehicle. Likewise, our kitchen table resting on four legs is much more stable than our three-legged plant stand. The number four grants a certain measure of stability; there is something unique to its particular expression. A table supported by one, two or even three legs is apt to tip quite readily. In contrast, a table with four legs is stable. Though a table with six, eight or ten legs would be even more stable, the additional number of legs sacrifices the spaciousness and openness of the form. What makes four special is that it is the smallest number required for stability of form. Any fewer parts decreases the stability, any more parts decreases the flexibility. With the number four there remains a certain measure of freedom and openness. So though we often think of the term "stable" as inflexible or perhaps even rigid, when applied to the number four it is more accurate to think of "stable" as support without sacrificing freedom of movement. This insight into the nature of "four" as a flexible measure of stability is important for our work with The Sacred Cross.

To explore the number four in a mythic sense, let us consider how it is used within the minor arcana of the Tarot. Interestingly, the fourth card within each suit represents or inspires a particular quality of stability. The Four of Wands offers insights into the stability of our passions and labors, while the Four of Cups speaks to the stability of emotions. The Four of Swords represents the stability of mind, while the Four of Pentacles guides us toward the stability of prosperity[6]. This

---

[6] Masino, Marcia. *Easy Tarot Guide*, ACS Publications, 1987.

same theme continues in traditional astronomy and astrology where an encircled equal armed cross is the glyph (or symbol) that is used to represent the planet Earth. The vertical line in the encircled cross represents a north/south meridian while the horizontal line represents the equator. As we know, the Earth provides the ground that serves as the stable foundation for our viewing and experiencing the Heavens.

The Four-fold Grace

Having discussed the qualities inherent within the equal armed cross, let us also speak to the synergy that occurs as a result of their convergence in the center of The Sacred Cross. To do so we must introduce what I like to call the trump card of all spiritual and magical practices: this word is "grace." Grace is the freely given, unmerited favor and love of the Divine. It is that which manifests unexpectedly in our lives as a result of *nothing* we've done to deserve it. Grace is the trump card that outdoes all our expectations and understandings of self-worth; it is through the gift of grace that we learn just how precious we are.

In the center of The Sacred Cross the four extended arms converge. This convergence catalyzes an action within us that can only be described as a "four-fold grace." This four-fold grace consists of the magical synergy of the combined powers and potentials of each of the four arms of The Sacred Cross. In keeping with the mystery known to its name, very little can be *said* about the nature of the four-fold grace generated within the heart of The Sacred Cross. This is in part because it comes in different ways to different people depending upon their needs; and in part because it is a felt sense that should not be concretized with words that might fix your expectations of its offering.

Before leaving the foundations section of this book, we should address a question that is often uttered when people are introduced to The Sacred Cross for the first time. As you know, sacred symbols mean different things to different people. For  some, the word "cross" conjures images of crucifixion and suffering as conveyed through some Christian teachings. Because this is so, at the beginning of our work it is important to make distinctions between the Calvary, Latin or sacrificial crosses currently used within the Christian tradition and the equal armed cross that serves as the geometrical foundation for The Sacred Cross.

In my research, I discovered the representations and associated meanings behind two hundred and sixty eight crosses of various forms recognized by a wide range of people living in the world today. If you take the time to research the various forms of the cross as I did, you will see that any slight change in form (addition or subtraction of an aspect) gives rise to a dramatic change in meaning. As we begin our journey with The Sacred Cross we must understand that because the geometrical intersection of four lines has been and is continually used in many different ways, we cannot assume that the meaning imposed upon one cross applies to any other. Because the sacrificial, Calvary or Latin cross pictured above is so widely recognized as the symbol of the Christian faith, it is important to explain how it differs from the equal armed Sacred Cross.

First and most obvious the two crosses are geometrically dissimilar. The sacrificial cross is composed of three equal arms and one longer arm, while The Sacred Cross is composed of four arms of equal length. Secondly, I will reiterate the fact that the representational use of the equal armed cross predates the representational use of the sacrificial, Calvary or Latin crosses. If you look into this distinction further, you will find that, given its associations with eternal life, the sacrificial cross was likely co-opted from the Egyptian ankh or crux ansata.

We know that the sacred geometrical form known as the equal armed cross is embedded within the arts and architecture of pre-Christian civilizations. We also know that within those contexts it is believed to express the sacred principles of the "harmony of four." In contrast, the sacrificial, Calvary or Latin cross is used to represent a very different principle which in its most positive state expresses as the union of Divinity or the Holy Trinity (three equal lines) and the world (long line) and in its most negative state serves as the justification for suffering as an exalted expression of the Christian faith.

I have been advised several times to consider changing the name of The Sacred Cross to something less fraught with potential misconception. Wouldn't it make more sense to forego pushing buttons of religious reactivity while endeavoring to teach a method aimed at aiding spiritual growth? While I can certainly understand and sympathize with this point of view, I have instead chosen to honor the name given to me by the Inner Contacts behind this tool as gesture of trust and reverence. Though reverence for its origins would be enough of a reason to keep the name as given, I would like to offer a second reason as well. It is simply this: I truly believe that we are all responsible for reclaiming the sacred words and phrases that have become tainted by the misuse and misunderstanding of others. I choose to use words like cross, priestess, ritual and pagan because I would rather be a part of their reclamation than a part of their continued and misappropriated shame.

If the idea of working with a cross is difficult for you, begin by thinking of The Sacred Cross as a meeting place, a "crossroads" or an intersection of four ways of being and knowing, versus a "cross." From here, please consider letting the four-fold grace inherent within this tool teach you the difference between the equal armed cross that radiates harmony, spacious stability and the strength of support, and the sacrificial cross that has for centuries been used to inspire suffering and martyrdom.

The Stream Behind The Sacred Cross

Before completing this section on the foundations of The Sacred Cross, I will relay another piece of information rarely shared about this tool. It comes from an experience I had working with the first Women of Vision[7] program in 2004. I will start by stating that the initial inspiration for this tool came to me in 2002 while meditating with the Inner Contacts associated with the Oversoul of PCA. At first, I received only

---

[7] The Women of Vision program is an Arab, Israeli and American partnership for women's personal and collective empowerment through use of personal and transformational ritual tools in a circle setting. This program was co-founded by Lila Sophia Tresemer, Dorit Bat Shalom (an Israeli peace worker, artist and performer) and myself in 2004.

the vertical arms of The Cross in the form of a spiraling pillar connecting Heaven and Earth through the human body. For a year, I worked with and taught this tool assuming it was the sum of the inspirational guidance. Between 2003 and 2004 the horizontal arms offered themselves as an augmentation to the vertical pillar and I began to work on the incorporated form for The Sacred Cross.

At the commencement of our first Women of Vision program in October 2004, The Sacred Cross was just beginning to be taught in its totality. Because it was still quite new, we were uncertain how it would work within a trans-religious/cultural circle. Thus we did not plan to include The Cross among the methods intended for the ten-day Women of Vision program. For many of our fourteen women, this was a once-in-a-lifetime experience, foreign in every way to that which they'd known. As we entered our third day, we realized that the individuals in our group would benefit greatly from an ability to ground themselves in this unfamiliar land as well as rediscover their inspiration for being in the U.S.A. for our gathering. The tool that best fit this need was The Sacred Cross. Though our methods were not yet as refined as they are today, the power behind The Sacred Cross was astonishing. The four-fold grace akin to its nature made itself known to each one of us, instructors and participants alike, in remarkable and revealing ways. One of the most remarkable revelations came through one woman's dream.

On the last day of the program, one of the Israeli women came to me desiring to share a dream she'd had the night before. Lying in bed trying to sleep, she found herself worrying about how she would be able to leave the peace she found in

Colorado and return to the challenges of her homeland. Ruminating on these concerns, she fell asleep. During the night, a powerful spirit woman came to her in a dream visitation. Our friend asked the spirit woman her lingering question, "How will I be able to return to the difficulties at home after an experience such as this?" At that moment, the spirit woman conjured the form and force of The Sacred Cross. Then she vigorously pushed both the form and the power it holds deep into our sister's body. With this, our friend received a sudden jolt, followed by a strong sense of balance, strength and peace. As the spirit woman turned to depart, our sister asked "Who are you?" The woman replied, "My name is Mary Magdalene." As she relayed this final piece to me the following day, a jolt went through my body, too. It was the first time I received an insight into the specific Inner Contacts behind the tool I had been working with for the past two years.

To be clear, the personal spiritual imprint available to us as Mary Magdalene is part of a collective or tribe. All human and spiritual beings possess their own spiritual affinities that bind them to their own tribe. As human beings we gravitate to persons who share our soul's calling; the same is true of our otherworldly allies. It is through spiritual affinities that we find our human friends/partners and non-human Inner Contacts across distances and lifetimes. The spiritual tribe, of which Mary Magdalene is one important expression, works through The Sacred Cross because its power is in alignment with the spiritual affinity of her life's work. Though she is the one who made herself known to our sister through the dream, her presence stands within a lineage that is dedicated to each person's direct knowing of God/Goddess and to sacred union as an expression of the Divine Feminine and Divine Masculine through the empowerment of love. It is this lineage of direct knowing and sacred union that informs the spiritual foundations of The Sacred Cross and of PCA. As I am endeavoring to reveal more of the history behind The Sacred Cross, I feel it is important to convey this story.

The Fallacy of Beginner's Tools

Before leaving this section defining the origins of The Sacred Cross, I would like to take a moment to dispel a popular misconception as it keeps many men and women of spirit entangled in false notions regarding their spiritual and magical practices. At the onset of our spiritual and magical pursuits we are introduced to the basic tools of the system we are endeavoring to learn. During these days of elementary training, we work hard to absorb the basics of our newly chosen path. Some new students believe that the goal is to quickly and thoroughly learn the "introductory" teachings/practices so that they may move beyond them to the more glamorous and complex teachings/practices that follow. This is a completely false assumption and one I invite all users of The Sacred Cross to wipe from their consciousness.

All spiritual and magical systems begin their trainings by focusing on the virtues of the basics of their tradition. Though taught at the beginning, these offerings are not merely "beginner's tools" to be mastered and excelled beyond. They are the bedrock upon which all the subsequent spiritual and magical practices are built. I cannot tell you how many times I've watched students bypass building the repetitious strength of a consistent foundational practice for the enticing call of the glamorous path, only to find out, in the end, that they've built a house of cards that any mild wind can topple. So, with their proverbial tails between their legs, they return to the foundations to fortify their structure and reclaim the strength and durability they'd sacrificed.

The foundational tools presented to us at the beginning of our spiritual and magical endeavors are put before us because it is they who will guide, challenge and support us for the rest of our lives. As opposed to thinking of them as the parents from whom we must eventually emancipate ourselves, we should think of these foundational tools as the bones of our body. If we were to venture into the world minus those structural friends, we would not be able to hold ourselves upright.

Because our foundational tools and skills keep us "upright" in our spiritual and magical work, we introduce The Sacred Cross early within the Level One Training. In this way our students begin their work possessing the strong spiritual bones that can and will support them throughout their work in PCA. As you venture forward in your spiritual and magical pursuits, remember this: the magic of our foundational tools and skills deepens and expands as the practice of the man or woman using it deepens and expands. With this as your orientation, you are in the best possible alignment to venture forward in your own work with The Sacred Cross. We will continue forward in our exploration by moving to *Part 2: The Physical and Metaphysical Elements of The Sacred Cross.*

Part 1: Questions for Contemplation

1. There were three primary virtues discussed in reference to the unique nature of The Sacred Cross as a spiritual and magical tool for our time. Can you name and briefly speak to each one?

2. What are the geometrical/spiritual foundations of this tool?

3. Relatively speaking, which aspect(s) of The Cross's foundation sparked the most questions or concerns for you? What can and will you do to investigate the answers to your questions?

4. Which aspect(s) of The Cross's foundations excite or interest you the most?

5. How specifically can you begin to imagine working with this tool within the context of your life?

Part 2: Physical and Metaphysical Elements of The Sacred Cross

Introduction to the Terms of Art Used Within

All spiritual and magical groups develop terms of art that speak to the specifics of their teachings, understandings and beliefs. In PCA, we use several terms of art specific to our work. To begin our exploration of the physical and metaphysical elements of The Sacred Cross, I will speak to and define the terms of art used in our work. As they may be entirely new to many readers, it is important to create common ground before delving into the specifics of The Cross. Once common ground is established, we will turn our attention toward the metaphysical mechanics of The Sacred Cross itself. As it serves as the foundation for all spiritual and magical practices, we will begin our term of art definitions with "stillness."

Stillness

As men and women of spirit, it is important for us to find a way to release all prior occupations and come into a place of mental, physical and emotional stillness. We do this at the beginning of our spiritual and magical workings, meditations and even at the beginning and ending of our day. If you are unfamiliar with the concept of a stillness practice and its place in the life of a man or woman of spirit, an explanation of its virtues may be useful.

In our normal waking life, we are physically active, emotionally engaged and, for the most part, less focused and aware spiritually. We spend the bulk of our days doing what we must do to survive in the physical world as a human being; this includes activities such as working, parenting, caretaking, cooking, driving, reading emails and the like. In these states of being we operate like little generators of energy, ideas, actions and words. Engaged in these activities, our thoughts, emotions and even physical bodies can become totally focused upon their current occupation. If, while in this state, someone interrupts us with important information, we have to stop, sit down, quiet our thoughts, or in other words turn the activity of our generator down (or off), before we are capable of directing our attentions toward them and that which they wish to share with us. The same process occurs when we enter into our spiritual and magical work. We have to purposefully stop our activities, still our bodies, quiet our minds so that we can actually listen to and hear that which our allies in the unseen worlds wish to share with us. To make this shift, men and women of spirit rely upon our stillness practices.

Stillness is a cultivated form of passive meditation. Its aim is to render us physically tranquil, emotionally calm and spiritually receptive. In this neutral and quiet state, our true perceptions of the otherworlds are given an environment that is supportive of their emergence. I say stillness is "cultivated" because it takes practice to learn how to shift ourselves out of our generator mode and into a tranquil, calm and receptive state for several minutes at a time. Because this is the case, early efforts to cultivate stillness through meditation can frustrate us. If this is so for you, do not despair; and by all means, do not give up the task for the benefits of a stillness practice are well worth the effort. As adepts within nearly all spiritual and magical traditions will attest, it is only in the stillness of our being that we are able to hear the voice of the Divine. Meaning, it is only when we quiet the frequency of our little personal generator that we can actually hear, sense, see and feel "another." For those of us not used to a stillness practice, I will offer two simple processes I often use with students who are new to this form of meditation.

As our spiritual and magical work develops, we will learn to sustain our awareness of the spirit worlds at all times. However, at the beginning of our spiritual and magical work, our waking orientation is primarily toward the manifest world, and not the inner worlds. One way persons new to the practice of stillness can build their aptitude for inner world work is by working with the natural tendencies of their five senses. As we know our senses are like the tentacles of a deep sea creature or the ever moving ears of a doe, in that they are constantly directed toward the object of our interaction or curiosity. Throughout the normal waking day our senses are directed, nearly exclusively, toward the outer world of form. In other words, they are focused upon what we are seeing, hearing, eating, smelling and tasting. Our five senses inform and delight us, keep us safe and allow us to interact with all we encounter in the physical world. In contrast, during sleep and meditation our five senses naturally reorient toward the innerworlds. As such they come into a relationship with our subconscious, our physical body, the spirit realms closest to the Earth and even, on occasion, the more exalted solar and stellar realms. Miraculously, these same five senses inform and delight us, keep us safe and allow us to interact with all we encounter in the otherworlds at night. Because they can be directed inwardly or outwardly, I have found that our five senses can be very helpful allies as we learn to cultivate stillness.

To repeat, our five senses are directed outwardly for the bulk of our day. During our sleep and meditation, these same senses shift away from their outer world orientation, migrating toward an inner world orientation. For some, this inward migration comes naturally as they perform their daily meditations or prepare for sleep, for others it does not. For those compelled to keep their senses oriented outward at all times, the purposefully inward redirection of each individual sense can be quite helpful.

To do this we can begin by imagining our senses are the five petals of a wild rose that, through a stillness enfolding, come to rest in a bud. Like us, the closed bud of the wild rose is still very much alive and well within the physical world; however, its petals (and our senses) are oriented inward. In this inward orientation we find that a great deal of space begins to open up as our expansive inner world unfolds. Let's walk through this stillness enfolding, sense by sense, so we have a clear idea of this process.

Beginning with your sense of sight, simply close your eyes in a gesture that withdraws your vision from the outer world of form. As you are reading, take a moment to actually experience this; purposefully take in the world around you, then close your eyes. Notice the dramatic difference between your experience of the world with your eyes open and your eyes closed. Though it takes a bit more practice to experience, the same dramatic effect is possible with each of the other four senses.

Continuing our journey, you can also enfold your sense of hearing. This is done by orienting your listening capacity away from the overt sounds around you and toward the delicate whispers within you. If you doubt this capacity, think back to a time when you sat in a meeting and were so absorbed in your own thoughts that you missed several words in the dialog taking place around you. Someone called your name with a question and you suddenly snapped back into the present moment aware of all you'd missed. As we know, our hearing migrates inward and outward all the time.

You may also withdraw your sense of touch away from its physical orientation and toward the soft caress of the subtle realms as well. With touch, what you will notice is the feeling or sensing body becomes less densely or overtly oriented, and more aware of the subtle majesty of a light breeze, the heat on your skin or the touch of beings and energies of the inner worlds.

To continue, you may direct your intertwined senses of smell and taste away from the physical world and toward the subtle octaves of the inner worlds. Here you will notice that you are able to move beyond the overt smell/taste you normally notice. Sometimes the presence of subtle tastes and smells are the product of shifts in our internal chemistry catalyzed by our spiritual and magical work. At other times they are the means by which otherworldly communications are sent to us. In this change, you will begin to notice the smells and tastes that exist within you and within the worlds.

With your five senses enfolded like the petals of a wild rose, allow the stillness that lives deep within you to arise. With its coming, you will notice that you have access to previously untapped sources of wisdom, clarity, rest and peace.

A second method for cultivating a meditative stillness relies upon the physical body, versus the extension of the body via the five senses. For those of us bathed in the nervous system stimulation of computers, cell phones, caffeine and sugar, the body seems to be racing all the time. Thus, it serves our journey into stillness to reconnect with the physical body itself. In this method our focus is upon the element of Earth. We do this by breathing in and out through the nose and by placing our awareness upon the Earth element within us: our bones. Moving beneath the constant firing of the nervous system, muscles and tendons we come into a relationship with the "scaffolding" of the physical body. Our focus in this meditation is the simple dance between our ever-flowing breath and ever-supportive bones.

Please note, tracks 1 and 2 on CD II offer the following stillness meditation sequence.

Stillness Meditation I

Imagine you are a wild rose...with your five petals, as senses extending into the world and reaching toward the sun. See this rose as you see yourself now, leaving the fullness of your life's engagement, in need of stillness. To find the stillness you seek, begin by relaxing the will forces that energize your outward extension. Starting with the extended petal of sight, simply close your eyes, drawing in that sense until the colors that surround you fade into quiet darkness. Enfold your petal of hearing... pulling your listening self away from the sounds around you and toward the "still, small voice" within you. Allow your sense of touch to leave the dense physical world and seek instead the delicate caress of the inner realms. Draw inward your senses of smell and taste so they too may experience the subtleties of the worlds within. Now enfolded, the petals of your flower draw themselves softly into a bud. It is within the stillness of this bud that the quiet visions, whispers, caresses, scents and nectars of the innerworlds are offered to you. Commune in the embrace of this inner stillness in silence.

When you are ready to come back into your waking consciousness, simply reverse the enfolding process and, one by one, redirect each one of the petals of your wild rose back toward the outer world of form.

Stillness Meditation II

Choosing stillness... breathe in and out through your nose. Come deep inside yourself...until you meet your bones. Feel their constant strength. See how they join to form the scaffolding that supports your entire physical body. Choosing stillness, allow the soft tissues of your body to let go and hang upon the quiet strength of your bones. Feel how the vigilance and alertness of your nerves, muscles and tendons relax into the silent majesty of your bones.

Choosing stillness...breathe in and out through your nose. Still deep inside...become aware of the whirling of the breath...dancing, weaving around and among the bones and all they support. Feel how this breath possesses the power to reorient you...to cleanse, to purify and to soothe you. Allow the dance of breath and bone to court you deeper into their stillness. Bone and breath...breath and bone...be here in the peaceful stillness they co-create.

When your time in stillness is complete, increase the pace of your breath. Like the bellows that fan a spark to flame, use your lungs to stir the winds within you that awaken the sleeping soft tissues, causing them to rise from their resting place. Refreshed and relaxed, open your eyes and return your full awareness to the outer world of form.

With this, we have touched upon the concept of meditative stillness relied upon in several places throughout this book. Following the invitation to stillness at the beginning of each Sacred Cross meditation or exercise, you will see/hear something like this: "using your will, attention and sacred imagination direct your awareness toward X"("X" being the particular step or focus of the meditation). As they logically follow stillness, let us take a moment to explain what is meant by the terms will, attention and sacred imagination in our work.

Will

The word "will" is used to describe the creative power within us. It is the conscious energy that we put forth when we engage ourselves in life, work, love, play and spiritual practices. In our spiritual practices the concept of will is very important, and unfortunately, often misperceived and misused. The nature of the misperception of will lies within our rejection or acceptance of our ongoing relationship with the Divine. If we accept ourselves as part of the Divine Intelligence from which the created world emanates, our understanding of will is as multifaceted as our understanding of Self. If, however, we do not believe that we are an expression of the Divine Intelligence, then our understanding of will is based solely on the strength of our humanity. In other words, if we live our lives knowing that we are part of the web of creation and can thus draw upon its resources, then our will is enhanced by these resources. If, in contrast, we live our lives believing that we are human beings living human lives in a human creation, then we are not open to nor can we draw upon the web of life. To deepen our appreciation of this distinction, let's turn to the words of the ancient Greek philosopher and mystic Plotinus.

> "So divine and so precious is The Soul, be confident that, by its power, you can attain to divinity. Start your ascent. Your will not need to search long. Few are the steps that separate you from your goal. Take as your guide the most divine part of The Soul, that which "borders" upon the superior realm from which it came....The Soul is no more than an image of The Intelligence. How is it, then, that Souls forget the divinity that begot them so that – divine by nature, divine by origin – they now know neither divinity nor self? The evil that has befallen them has its source in self-will, in being born, in becoming different, in desiring of independence. Once having tasted the pleasures of independence, they use their freedom to go in a direction that leads them away from their origin."[8]

What Plotinus is saying to us is simple. To come into life, we must accept our incarnation and, in that, separate from the higher realms of the Divine. Once separate we begin to experience life on Earth and all of the joys and pleasures of being embodied. However, if instead of allowing that joy to rekindle our appreciation of and connection to the Divine, we simply fixate on corporeal pleasures, our will forces become relegated to a humanocentric, or Soul-less, source point. In this, we lose our connection to the truth of our origins and the Divine Will itself. Living this life, we think that we must figure things out alone, fight the good fight, stand as the lone defender of what's right and push ourselves against the grain with our "will." Performing spiritual and magical work with this

---

[8] O'Brien, Elmer. *The Essential Plotinus*. Hackett Publishing Company, Indianapolis, Indiana, 1964, pp. 91-92.

consciousness, we condition ourselves to employ our will toward the achievement of success, ease from pain, finding of love, better health and the like. And we wonder why this doesn't work?

One single phrase used at the conclusion of prayers and ceremonies alike guides us toward right relationship between our own will and the Divine will. It is this: "if it be in the Highest Good, let my request be received and granted." Encased within this phrase is the understanding that as sons and daughters of the Divine, our true will, or creative power, is sourced from the confluence of our human self and Divine self. This is the meaning behind the word "will" in our work. Again, it is the creative power that finds its source in the confluence of our human will and the Divine will working in concert. While on the subject of will, I would like to make one additional point with regard to the misappropriated use of the term; this time I will contest the other end of the spectrum.

Often when students of metaphysical practices are complimented for their good works, they reply "Oh, it was not me…it was God/Goddess/Buddha/Isis moving through me. I give total credit to them." To this, I always reply "Nonsense!" for any other reply negates the truth of the matter. While I recognize the beauty and humility of statements of veneration like the one just referenced, I take exception with the foundation upon which they are based, for I believe this demonstrates a fundamental lack of understanding. When we work as men and women of spirit we work in partnership with the beings and energies of the unseen worlds. The word partnership implies mutual work for mutual benefit. If we offer ourselves benevolently for the good of any other person, place or thing as part of our sacred service, we are engaging in the physical act that constitutes our part in these partnerships. In turn, our spiritual allies are offering their energetic inspiration and support toward the completion of the same. To negate either the human or non-human aspect of this partnership is to commit a spiritual blunder. Before we can become practitioners of the sacred we must learn to correctly attribute the powers at work within and beyond us. The beings and energies of the unseen worlds offer us many wonderful things such as inspiration, energy, guidance and love, but it is we who must meditate, raise the ritual chalices and stroke the head of a sick friend so that the spiritual medicine our allies carry can find passage into the world of form.

In all things we retain some measure of the gift of choice; and it is through the vehicle of our free will that we exercise that choice. Please remember, in our work with The Sacred Cross the term "will" is used to describe the creative power we possess and offer in alignment with the sacred partnerships we've chosen to create. And in this, we must learn to honor our part, the unseen world's part and the synergy of the whole.

Attention

The word "attention" also has a specific meaning in the context of our work with The Sacred Cross. Attention is the act of directing our mind, senses and/or thoughts upon a specific thing. Our attention focuses the occupation of our mental and sensory consciousness. We all direct and redirect our attention hundreds of time each and every day, but few of us have actually stopped to unpack the dynamic interplay of our own attention. Because it affects our spiritual and magical work a great deal, in PCA we spend a significant amount of time exploring the application of our attention. Through this pursuit, we have discovered how best to work with our attention in a spiritual and magical context.

First, it is important that we understand how our attention actually functions. Our attention consists of many small, and somewhat independent, increments of consciousness. In PCA we like to call these increments "attention particles." When we choose to focus our attention on something like a beautiful tree in our garden, we place a certain amount of our free and available attention particles upon that tree. What is interesting is the fact that we can focus attention particles upon the beautiful tree while simultaneously focusing our other attention particles upon a phone conversation we're having with a friend. Many of us have become quite skilled at spreading the particles of our attention among several things at once. How many of us have mastered the art of cooking dinner while talking on the phone and watching our three year old play on the living room carpet? What about this example: driving a car while talking on a cell phone and drinking a hot cup of coffee? When our attention is simultaneously diffused among several different occupations, we are engaged in the beloved 21st century activity known as "multi-tasking." While multi-tasking may assist us to keep pace with the demands placed upon us during our waking life, it does not, in any way, assist us in our spiritual and magical work. For this, we must condense the particles of our attention in favor of a singular focus. Why? Because the more attention particles we focus upon any one thing, the more powerful the circuit of force (connection, magnetism or affinity) becomes between us and that thing; likewise, the fewer we focus, the weaker the circuit of force.

When performing our meditations, rituals and prayers our aim is to concentrate the bulk of our available attention particles upon the work at hand. In doing so, we establish a strong circuit of force between us, our unseen allies and our spiritual work. If an active leak exists in our attention field (e.g. if our particles become scattered away from our work), the circuit of force weakens and the power of our work wanes.

Thus far I have been speaking to the importance of uniting and focusing our attention particles when engaged in our spiritual and magical work. This point withstanding, do not let the notion of focused attention give rise to the belief that your consciousness must function in a rigid and unyielding manner. In the context of spiritual and magical work, a focused attention is never rigid or unyielding. In fact, those states of consciousness decrease our ability to perceive the subtleties of the otherworlds. Rather, as men and women of spirit our goal is to learn how to place half of our attention particles upon our spiritual and magical work while the other half are poised to receive otherworldly feedback in response. The balanced sacred union of male and female forces within us can be a helpful way to envision how this works.

To begin, we must place half of our attention particles upon the intention of our spiritual work (e.g. to pray for a sick relative, to honor the full moon, shift a limiting belief within us or perform a baby blessing ritual, etc.) Because it involves a certain degree of assertion, we can think of this first stage as the masculine manner of employing our attention. From here, we place the other half of our attention particles upon our sacred imagination and subtle body. We do this because these are the primary vehicles through which we perceive and receive the subtle messages of the unseen worlds. As it requires a certain degree of receptivity, this is the feminine manner of employing our attention. Together the acts of masculine focus and feminine reception co-create a balanced, whole-body conscious "attention" to our spiritual and magical work. Over the years I have learned that this complementary active and receptive focus of our attention particles produces the best results. As we move into the invocation phase of our work with The Sacred Cross, do your best to aim for this same balanced state of focused attention within you. From attention, let us move now to the final term of art used in our work with The Sacred Cross.

Sacred Imagination

Our last term of art is "sacred imagination." In our work, this phrase is used to describe the elevated, creative faculties within our mental body. Let me explain what I mean by the "elevated, creative faculties." The human imagination can be used in a number of ways ranging from ultra positive to ultra negative. In the positive sense, we possess the capacity to devote our imaginative faculties to building thoughts and images that promote healing, love, growth and harmony in ourselves and in the world. In the negative sense, we possess the capacity to devote our imaginative faculties to building thoughts and images that promote hatred, anger, vengeance and discord in ourselves and in the world. By using the term "sacred imagination" I am endeavoring to focus us upon the positive, elevated and creative end of our human imaginative spectrum. For it is this aspect of our creative mental body that we should bring to our spiritual and magical work.

The sacred imagination is one of two primary means of communication between seen and unseen worlds. The other means is the subtle body receptivity to subtle messages and impulses just discussed as the feminine gesture of attention. In our spiritual and magical work both means are equally important. Use of the sacred imagination in our spiritual and magical work occurs in two ways: 1) *giving communication* to the unseen world through the projection of creative thoughts and 2) *getting communication* from the unseen worlds through the reception of imagery. Let us briefly speak to both.

In the first context, the sacred imagination is used to give or offer communication from our human consciousness outward to the consciousness of the otherworldly beings or energies with whom we wish to engage. Though it houses the beginning of sacred imagination's creative process, the mind is not where the power of our sacred imagination begins and ends. As the seat of the sacred imagination, our mind is where we start to build our ritual, prayer and meditative images. Once built with the creative capacity of our mind, the aim is to offer or project these images outward, beyond the physical world and into the shared space between the worlds of force and form. Remember, we are physical beings bound, for the most part, to the world of form; however, the beings of the unseen worlds are not. Thus, to interact and commune with one another, we must find one another within the shared energetic space of the subtle realms that hover between the physical world and the unseen worlds. Our projection of thoughts, prayers, meditative images and the like places aspects of our consciousness in the shared space between the worlds where different forms of intelligence can communicate together. In doing this, we are, in essence, placing our human "calling card" onto the silver platter that announces our arrival in the shared space of the subtle realms. As there is no universal common language, information is shared in the form of image, color, tone and energy, all of which are harbored within the sacred imagery of the mind. Again, the first object of our use of the sacred imagination is to formulate and project our thoughts, prayers and visualizations.

The second aspect of the use of our sacred imagination comes through the strength of our stillness practice; for it is in this state of being that we are able to receive the clear communication given to our sacred imagination from our unseen allies. Once we have projected our thoughts, prayers and visual images into the shared space between the worlds, we simply wait in stillness for the image, color, tone or energy response to return to us. Sometimes this happens immediately, sometimes is comes days later. As you can imagine, having a clean sacred imagination is important before this step in the communication process can work properly. If our minds are cluttered with the graphic imagery generated by modern day television, computer games, interactive web tools and the like, it is hard for us to accurately receive and pictorially interpret the communication given to our sacred imagination by our unseen allies. This is due to the fact that our brain is used to having imagery generated for it by an outside source firing fast and furious toward its sensing capacity; thus it has lost the ability to generate imagery itself in response to inner or outer creative stimulus. Though there are many reasons to limit the amount of electronic imagery we take in, damage to our sacred imagination is something to seriously consider when we determine we wish to devote ourselves to the sacred arts.

With an understanding of stillness, will, attention and the sacred imagination under our belts, we are now ready to move onward to an exploration of the metaphysical mechanics of The Sacred Cross.

The Metaphysical Mechanics of The Sacred Cross

In this section, our focus turns toward developing an intellectual and experiential understanding of the The Sacred Cross. To do this, we will explore each of its five components in turn. My aim is to ensure a common orientation and understanding with regard to the metaphysical mechanics of each aspect of The Sacred Cross before we invoke the power of the whole. Before stepping into this territory, it is important to take note of the ground beneath our feet. Toward this end, I will briefly address some of the fundamental concepts central to the metaphysical mechanics of The Sacred Cross.

The Relevance of Location to Consciousness

As you will soon experience, as we begin our invocation of The Sacred Cross, we bring the fullness of our attention into our heart. From here we expand through the sphere that is our physical body system in search of the dwelling place of the powers that infuse the vertical arms of The Sacred Cross before delving deep within ourselves where the origins of the horizontal arms dwell. In the guidance for the invocation of the vertical arms, you will notice that I use the phrases "deep Earth" and "high Heavens." Though important in terms of orienting our consciousness, it must be clearly understood that these phrases do not refer to a form of spiritual hierarchy. Instead, these phrases are meant to instill an appreciation between ourselves and the greater world within which we live.

Because it is vitally important to our understanding of the way spiritual and magical works actually function, I will expand upon this notion in a rudimentary or step-by-step fashion.

Men and women of spirit are taught that at the commencement of any spiritual or magical work we must take a moment to claim our starting place, both physically and spiritually. We will, for instance, mindfully think or say aloud "I begin in my body with the East behind me and the West before me; to my right is the North and to my left is the South. In this place I begin my spiritual work." This acknowledgement of our state and location is important because it marks the place from which we step forth into the worlds of shared consciousness; furthermore, it is the place to which we will also return. The combination of our physical body system and its particular directional/elemental orientation co-creates a particular alchemy that informs and impacts our personal sphere and our work. For some, the terms "physical body system" or "personal sphere" may be new, so I will explain their use.

Many of us assume that our arms, legs, fingers, torso, bones, organs, skin, head and so on, are both the parts and parcel of our human body. Those of us engaged in metaphysical work and alternative healing therapies know that there is more to the human being that the physical body we can see, touch or have X-rayed at the doctor's office.

Just beyond the physical components of our bones, tissues, fingers, toes, skin and so forth are the energetic components of the subtle bodies that also comprise who we are. There is literally more to us than meets the eye. There are several schools of thought with regard to the specifics of the subtle bodies. Some schools work with four subtle bodies and some with seven, while others endeavor to work with as many as twelve subtle bodies. If you take the time to research these various systems, you will find that while differences in distinction do exist, most systems refer to the four major distinctions of the physical, etheric, astral and mental bodies.

No matter what system is used, it is clear that human beings are composed of a physical body we can see and a composite of subtle bodies we can sense. Though each of our subtle bodies is quite fascinating in its own right, I find it counterproductive to become too wed to the appeal of their separate distinctions. For when we do become wed to the parts, to use an old axiom, "often we can't find the forest for the trees." To avoid the pitfall of parts thinking and a rather over-intellectualized dissection of our humanity, it is far more helpful to think of our physical and subtle bodies as an amalgamated physical body system. When we think of ourselves as a physical body system, we are not only speaking with greater accuracy, but we are conditioning our minds to be better able to decode our interactions with the subtle forces of the unseen worlds.

Our physical body system is ordered in such a way that it graduates outward in a radiating sphere-like fashion. In the center of the field is the dense physical body and the closely situated etheric body; further out we find the astral body and the 'close to far' interweaving action of the mental body. Before, I said all spiritual and magical work begins with our orientation to self and the directions/elements around us; now we have further defined the self to include the amalgamation of the physical and subtle bodies which together comprises our physical body system or personal sphere. As it truly is our home starting place from which all spiritual and magical work begins and to which it ends, from this point forward I will refer to "our sphere;" you will know that it refers to the human physical body system.

Most of the time we engage ourselves in activities that occur within, around or otherwise close to our sphere. However, when we perform our spiritual and magical work, we extend our awareness and energies beyond our sphere by projecting our creative consciousness outward toward the "in between" places of consciousness and the larger spheres within which we also live. Let's take a moment to explore how this is done.

As a human being I live in my own personal sphere; however this sphere exists within the greater sphere of planet Earth. The greater sphere of planet Earth is composed of the atmospheric layer above it, the surface world upon it and the subsurface world within it. The Earth is thus a rather large sphere within which we live. Likewise, our Earth exists within the greater sphere created by the orbit of the Moon around and around the planet. Both Earth and Moon exist within the still greater sphere of the Solar System. Finally the Solar System exists within the vast sphere of the other stars and galaxies that co-create the Universe. In our work with The Sacred Cross, it is important to know both our place in our personal sphere and how our sphere is positioned within and thus relates to the greater spheres that encompass us. The diagram that follows illustrates the relationship between all the spheres I've just described.

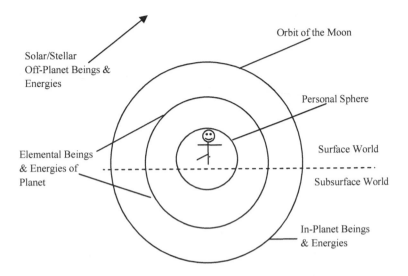

Solar/Stellar
Off-Planet Beings &
Energies

Orbit of the Moon

Personal Sphere

Elemental Beings
& Energies of
Planet

Surface World

Subsurface World

In-Planet Beings
& Energies

Like ripples in a pond cast forth by a single stone's plop, the spheres of our self, Earth, Moon, the Solar System and the Universe ripple outward in an ever-expanding array of concentric circles. And it is within these concentric circles that we actually live our lives. Though some of us confine our existence to that which is experienced within the human sphere alone, men and women of spirit live their lives aware of the greater spheres of life and consciousness that exist all about us. In some ways, this is the fundamental distinction between those that believe in and thus experience magic and those that do not. As beliefs have the ability to condition our consciousness, they possess a great deal of power indeed. If we think our life is limited to our simple human story and this story exists in the human sphere, we are not likely to be touched by the spirits alive within a redwood forest, the soft breath of the moon's nightly caress or the brilliant heart-warming tones of the radiant sun.

44

To assist our PCA students to grasp the magnitude of the concentric spheres within which we live and how our acclimation to them creates a magical consciousness within us, we teach a tool called *The Concentric Circles Model*[9]. Through this tool, our students begin to appreciate the graduated relativity of their own human stories. As an understanding of graduated relativity is important to all spiritual and magical work, a quick dive into *The Concentric Circles Model* will assist us.

The Concentric Circles Model uses the concept of expanding spheres to illustrate how our view and experience changes depending upon the current state or position of our consciousness. Using the relational approach inherent within the tool itself, we teach men and women of spirit how shifts in consciousness (e.g. within the spheres of existence) can shed new light on an old story. The following quote from Gareth Knight's forward for Dion Fortune's *The Training and Work of an Initiate* attests to the importance of this skill:

> "This is to say, (one must develop) a consciousness that looks upon the vicissitudes and challenges of daily life from a higher standpoint than the Lower Self or personality, with its genetic and environmental patterning. This is by no means a denial of the values of the ordinary life of the senses, emotions and lower mind, but an ability to see them in a broader context and to act accordingly[10]." - Gareth Knight

---

[9] The Concentric Circles Model was created by PCA Co-founder, facilitator Lila Sophia Tresemer who holds all copyrights for this material.
[10] Knight, Gareth. Forward to Dion Fortune's *The Training & Work of an Initiate*, Weiser Books, Boston MA, 2000.

The following diagram maps *The Concentric Circles Model* used in PCA.

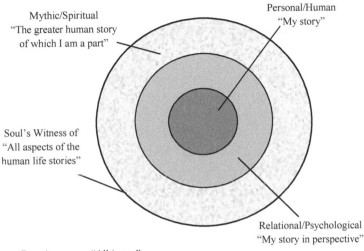

Mythic/Spiritual
"The greater human story
of which I am a part"

Personal/Human
"My story"

Soul's Witness of
"All aspects of the
human life stories"

Relational/Psychological
"My story in perspective"

Pure Awareness "All is one"

To explain how it works, let's begin by placing ourselves in the center circle where we are enfolded within the purely human view afforded us in the smallest space defined by our personal sphere. It is here that we experience and react to our life circumstances with our purely human consciousness (i.e. what Gareth Knight calls our "genetic and environmental patterning"). From the center circle, we can choose to expand outward until we come into contact with the psychological/relational sphere that encompasses our human sphere. In this sphere we encounter a different field of consciousness. This relational or philosophical field grants us a bit more perspective on our life's circumstances, thus enabling us to better understand and appreciate them. From this second sphere, we can expand outward again until we encounter the mythic sphere of consciousness, which encompasses both our human story and relational understanding. This sphere connects us to the greater human mythos within which all human stories are enfolded. Expanding even further outward, we meet the borderline where the soul or Higher Self witnesses the life from its place in the spirit realms. Expanding one final time, we move further into the space beyond the spheres where pure spiritual awareness enfolds it all.

As we expand from the center concentric sphere outward, our consciousness also expands and changes. Because our consciousness changes, the story itself also changes. Any one of these concentric circles is available to us at all times. It is up to us to choose to expand and contract our consciousness so that we may encounter and receive the gift that each sphere offers us. The same is true in our spiritual and magical work. There are spheres and fields of consciousness that exist beyond our own. Each is populated with the consciousness of many different beings and energies. Many of these beings and energies possess the power to gift us, elevating our sense of our self as well as our self in relationship to the beauty and wonder of the creative world. These realms exist independent of our acknowledgement of them; yet our acknowledgement is the key that opens the doors to magic between us and them. As magic is a conversation between different forms of intelligence or between beings that reside within different spheres, we must first *connect* before we can *converse*.

With this, our stage is finally set. Now, using terminology specific to The Sacred Cross, let's return to our initial exploration of the relevance of location to consciousness.

Previously I mentioned that in our work with The Sacred Cross I use the terms "deep Earth" and "high Heavens." Further I stated that in doing so I am not aiming to create images of spiritual hierarchies in our sacred imaginations. Now we know that instead, I am referring to the same principles of relational relativity as were used in *The Concentric Circles Model* just described. In doing so I am affirming and opening the pathway to experience beings and energies that reside within the greater spheres of Earth and Heaven that exist beyond our sphere. In this context, the phrase "deep Earth" refers to the sphere of the Earth which includes its physical elements as well as the intra-planetary spiritual beings and energies that reside within it. By the same token, the phrase "high Heavens" refers to the spiritual elements, beings and energies that exist beyond the Earth or off-planet.

To invoke The Sacred Cross, or any other spiritual or magical tool that puts us in direct contact with the unseen realms, we must learn to expand our consciousness beyond our personal sphere and toward the greater spheres within which we also dwell. For unless we exercise our ability to move beyond our self, we can never truly hope to find another.

There is one more important element to incorporate into our discussion on the relevance of location to consciousness. It is related to our earlier discussion of the sacred imagination and the importance of building images *with* our minds and not *in* our minds. As you begin to enhance your relationships with the beings and energies that exist beyond your personal sphere, you must remember this statement made previously in this section: our spiritual and magical work does not validate the existence of any of the other spheres beyond us; these spheres and their inhabitants exist whether or not we choose to connect to them. Though others may live their lives unaware of the spheres of the otherworlds, men and women of spirit acknowledge their existence. Further, our aim is beyond simple acknowledgement, for we seek to create a life that weaves matter and energy harmoniously between the spheres. If we wish to establish communion with other reservoirs of life, we have to reach beyond ourselves and go out to meet them. Once we've established contact with the elements, beings and energies of the other spheres, we can begin to learn how to co-creatively partner with them.

This notion of partnering and weaving is most important for us today. As humans, I believe that a disproportionate number of our spiritual foibles manifest through our patronage of ridiculously complex spiritual and magical methods we think we should be performing. Our New Age bookstores are filled with complicated spells, incantations, ritual workings and the like. Many are authored by persons who have no real spiritual or magical experience, but are instead seeking to capitalize on a burgeoning market. Maybe there was a time when scripts and complex ceremonial designs were necessary and helpful to bring humanity back into its relationship with the greater spheres. But in all humility, I must assert that I believe that time is past. Now is the time for simple methods that help us build working relationships between ourselves and the other benevolent forms of consciousness that exist all around us all the time. Now is the time to recycle our dogma and replace it with the simplicity of our own, personal and direct means of relating to the unseen worlds. In this context I must say that as a long time seer, I often feel the ache of the Inner Contacts who long for their human partners to lay down their glamorous accouterments, imposing costumes and competitive hierarchies to simply stop, drop and listen to their own inner guidance with a sincere desire to co-create. As I have said, via our spherical relationship, all forms of intelligence are already living together all the time. When we remember our interconnectedness and act from that remembrance, we are capable of co-creating real and enduring magic that stems from our knowing and caring for the unified fields of creation. Because its entire focus is on relationship and not some overburdening and complex methodology, The Sacred Cross is an ideal tool to assist men and women of spirit in the work that is being asked of us today.

The Virtues of Contraction as Well as Expansion

I have just spent considerable time attesting to the virtues of expanding beyond our sphere in an effort to commune with the beings and energies of the other spheres within which we live. However, expansion is only part of the picture; because it is vital to the cycles of life, we must also consider the virtues of contraction.

Life consists of cycles of expansion and contraction…birth and death…rising and falling. In PCA we believe it is through the fullness of these cycles of expansion and contraction that we learn to birth the Divine human being we truly are. Like the inflation and deflation of our lungs, the rise and fall of the seasons, the birth and death of a love relationship or the active and sleeping parts of our day, cycles of expansion and contraction are constantly present in our lives. As such, they are also important aspects of our spiritual and magical work.

In our invocation of The Sacred Cross we experience a balanced relationship between the forces of expansion and contraction. When we invoke the vertical arms of The Cross we do so through a wave-like motion that flows outward in a gesture of expansion and then contraction. In this, we expand beyond our sphere to commune with the forces of the high Heavens (off-planet) and the deep Earth (in-planet). From here, a contractive, focalizing motion brings these forces into a concentrated physical and energetic relationship with our sphere. In other words, we reach outward to that which exists beyond our sphere and then draw a concentrated beam from that place back to us.

In contrast, in our invocation of the horizontal arms the gesture works the other way. The elements that comprise the horizontal arms exist within our personal sphere for they are qualities and attributes we possess. Thus to invoke the horizontal arms, we first contract into our own sphere, conjuring our own essence, and then we expand outward offering this essence to ourselves and others.

To repeat, the vertical arms are invoked with a gesture of expansion to contraction, while the horizontal arms are invoked with a gesture of contraction to expansion.

Per this theme, I would like to touch upon one other important point with regard to the form. While the invocation of the vertical arms specifically orients us upwards to the Heavens and downwards to the Earth, the invocation of the horizontal arms is determined by the individual. As you will soon discover, one of the horizontal arms is oriented to "Who You Are" and the other to "What You Know." You will notice in the instructions for the invocation of these arms that neither is attributed specifically. Where the vertical arms are clearly specified as "up" and "down", the horizontal arms are not specified as "right" and "left." Why is there less specificity for the horizontal arms than for the vertical arms? The points of Earth and Heaven are fixed, relative to our sphere's location on the surface of the Earth; Heaven is off planet and Earth is upon and within planet. In contrast, "Who We Are" and "What We Know" dwell inside us. As we invoke our Sacred Cross, we must open to our bodily wisdom. This wisdom will tell us whether we naturally orient the arm of "Who I Am" to our right or our left side. Once the position for "Who I Am" is defined, the position for "What I Know" follows. It is important that we understand why "Who We Are" determines "What We Know." In life we begin by learning "Who We Are" as a person. Our features and personalities develop when we are young, as do our affinities and passions. From here, we determine how to fulfill all these aspects of "Who We Are" by developing the skills and tools that help us to best express ourselves in the world. As in life, so it is in our work with The Sacred Cross.

The Creative Tension of the Polarities

We are all familiar with the concept referred to as "creative tension" in one form or another. Some of us feel the creative tension between our work and family lives, our feminine and masculine inner self, while others feel the creative tensions between the Sun and Moon in the Heavens. No matter what the particulars, we are all familiar with the dynamic interplay between two seemingly opposing forces whose equally strong pull stretches us in new and different ways. Why am I mentioning this concept in the context of The Sacred Cross?

Because the dynamic interplay within the vertical arms links us to one of the most profound sources of creative tension that a human being can experience: the creative tension between Heaven and Earth. In its essence, the creative tension between Heaven and Earth is simply an energetic expression of the polarity between the forces of the Heavenly realms and the forces of the Earthly realm as felt by the human being situated in between. And as is the case in our other experiences of the same, the creative tension of these two polarities offers us a chance to stretch toward a place within us where the dual pull of Heaven and Earth harmonizes and co-exists.

Whatever your relationship to creative tension has been in the past, I encourage you to allow yourself to fully experience the initial tension between Earth and Heaven as you begin invoking the vertical arms of The Cross. I say this because our opening to this particular creative tension yields significant spiritual and magical benefits. I will speak to this tension and its benefits more fully in the chapter outlining the esoteric aspects of The Sacred Cross. For now, I want to be sure you understand that an initial sensation of creative tension between "opposing forces" in our work with The Sacred Cross is natural and actually quite beneficial. Do not avoid this tension or label it as a discomfort. Instead, acknowledge it and then open yourself to experience the transformation that naturally occurs when the tension between the poles resolves toward harmony. The "tension to harmony" experience is an essential part of the expression of The Sacred Cross. For wrapped within it is one of the greatest gifts this tool offers, as you will soon learn.

Once the four-fold grace of Earth, Heaven, "Who You Are" and "What You Know" begins to co-mingle within the heart, the creative tension eases. At this point, the wholeness of The Sacred Cross starts to fill the personal sphere of the practitioner. Once our sphere is filled, it becomes a reservoir for the continual flow of the four-fold grace of Earth, Heaven, "Who We Are" and "What We Know" for the duration of our invocation. In this action, it operates in an inward and outward flowing manner. First, The Cross brings the four-fold grace into our sphere and surrounding area, and then it lifts any residues, exhaustion or devitalizing energies out and away. Imagine, if you will, a portal or vessel through which energies flow both ways: into the field of working and out from the field of working. The inflow and outflow is moderated by the consciousness of your own heart's wisdom in concert with the knowing of the four-fold grace.

Now that we have a sense of the metaphysical mechanics of whole form, let us begin an exploration of the five components of The Sacred Cross, both generally and personally. Once you have been introduced to each of the five components of The Sacred Cross, you will be ready to invoke The Sacred Cross in its totality. As the heart is the moderator of The Sacred Cross, it is only fitting that we begin our discovery here.

The Heart

The human heart functions as the center of The Sacred Cross. In this role it is both the initiator and mediator of the four-fold grace as well as the center of consciousness for the physical body system. As this role contains both physical and metaphysical aspects, let us discuss each characteristic of the heart's occupation as the point of confluence in The Sacred Cross. To do this we will begin with the rudimentary understanding of the heart's function and then progress toward the lesser known polarity function of this magnificent organ.

In most medical textbooks we read, the heart is outlined as an organ of central importance for the physical body, in that it is the vessel through which blood is circulated outward to and returned from the whole human body. Further, every blood vessel and organ within in our entire physical body is said to rely upon the pumping action of the heart.

Contrary to the "National Anthem" pose which orients us to our heart through the placement of our right hand on the left side of our sternum, the heart is actually located in the center of the body in the middle of the thorax. The reason we mistakenly associate the heart with the left side of the body is because the left ventricle's pumping action is stronger than the right ventricle's action; consequently, we feel our heartbeat more strongly on the left side. The left and right sides of our heart perform different functions. The right side of our heart collects de-oxygenated blood from the body and the left side pumps out blood that has been re-oxygenated via our lungs.

Through the giving and receiving of blood, the substance of our vital life force, the heart allows the body to live, grow, heal and transform. The very same giving and receiving function is mirrored in center of The Sacred Cross, for it is the vessel within which the inflow and outflow of the four-fold grace of Earth, Heaven, "Who We Are" and "What We Know" takes place. When we consider the fact that the electromagnetic field of the heart has been measured to radiate at least 12-15 feet beyond the body, we begin to understand more fully why the heart is meeting place and moderator of the four-fold grace.

Within the 20st century, a new concept called Polarity Therapy was introduced by Dr. Randolph Stone (1890-1981). Based on scientific data used to analyze its true function, Stone theorized that the heart is not a pump at all. In fact, all the evidence he considered seemed to negate the established medical understanding that the heart has enough force as a muscle to accomplish the task of pumping the volume of blood that is actually circulated throughout the body. In a well researched article written by John Chitty, RPP, RCST called *The Heart is not a Pump*,[11] Stone's theory of the heart's function is summarized:

> "The cadence itself is the subject of inquiry, serving as a sort of metronome to which many other functions orient[12]. But greater interest arises as the inquiry turns to more subtle levels. The true function of the heart is to regulate the polarity action (cycles of inward and outward pulsation) of the primary energy field of the body. Furthermore, this polarity action is the foundation of the physical, emotional and psychological well-being; therefore the heart's role is a central, perhaps the central, esoteric function at the foundation of health...Because the polarized cycle of expansion and contraction is the fundamental engine for all phenomena, the 'glue of the universe[13]' the heart's activity can be characterized as the subtle basis for all health"

Because they are pivotal to our understanding of the heart as the center of The Sacred Cross, let's repeat two key phrases from the paragraph just quoted: "The true function of the heart

---

[11] Chitty, John. RPP, RCST. *The Heart is not a Pump*. www.energyschool.com.
[12] Pearsall, Paul. M.D. *Heart's Code*, Broadway Books, New York, 1998.
[13] Zukav, Gary. *The Dancing Wu-Li Masters*. William Morrow & Co. NY, 1979.

is to regulate the polarity action of the primary energy field of the body...because the polarized cycle of expansion and contraction is the fundamental engine for all phenomena, the 'glue of the universe[14]' the heart's activity can be characterized as the subtle basis for all health." These statements bear special interest to us as practitioners of The Sacred Cross. We already understand that The Cross creates a meeting place for the harmonized polarity of Heaven/Earth and Who We Are/What We Know, or our Divine self and our human self, within the physical body system. We also know that The Cross incorporates the primal currents of expansion and contraction in its initial invocation and subsequent spiritual/magical action. Finally, we understand that the dynamic interplay among the forces of Earth, Heaven, Who We Are and What We Know co-creates the unique and powerful four-fold grace of The Sacred Cross. This four-fold grace is capable of healing, uplifting, purifying, cleansing, fortifying, informing and energizing us and the space around us. How wonderful that the human heart possesses the very same harmonizing and regulating capacities within its own physical and energetic make up. It is even more remarkable when I reveal that I did not know anything about Stone's Polarity Theory until my seventh year of working with this tool. I was teaching a class on The Sacred Cross and one of the men in the class brought this revolutionary scientific understanding of the heart to my attention.

Beyond the physical rationale just relayed, there are metaphysical reasons justifying the heart as the center of The Sacred Cross. Metaphysically speaking, the human heart is to the body like the Sun is to the Solar System in which we live.

---

[14] Zukav, Gary. *The Dancing Wu-Li Masters.* William Morrow & Co. NY, 1979.

The Sun is the central and most powerful creative force within our Solar System. It is the nearest stellar being to which we humans have direct, daily access both physically and spiritually. Without the Sun, we would not physically exist. Comparatively, the heart is the center of the entire physical body system. I would argue that, akin to the Sun's position in our Solar System, the heart is the most powerful creative force within the human body system. Certainly we could not exist without it. Taking another metaphysical step, we look to the sacred patterns of the Qabalah which deepen the relationship between the life force of the Sun and the life force of our human heart; this again strengthens the place the heart holds as the center of The Sacred Cross.

In Qabalah, the Sun resides within the sixth sephirah called Tiphareth or Beauty. As we view the Tree of Life following this paragraph, we see Tiphareth (colored in grey below) is central within the form. In his book, *The Miracle Tree*, R.J. Stewart tells us the sixth sephirah "embodies the forces of beauty, harmony, balance and the Sun which is the greater being within which we have our Earthly life. The Sun mediates the spiritual power of Harmony and Balance from the universal realm of Being, into the specific realm of the Solar System."[15] The Sun's place is further explained by noted scholar, Rabbi Joseph Gikatilla in his book *Gates of Light*, when he says "Tiphareth is the sphere to which the upper and lower spheres

---

[15] Stewart, R.J. *The Miracle Tree*, New Page Books, 2003.

cling…it is the one that brings the spheres together with its letters."[16]

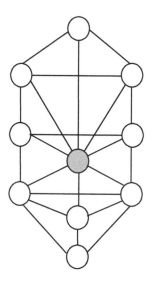

Metaphysically speaking, in constructing The Sacred Cross, we begin in the heart because our heart is the Sun within our body[17], in that, spiritually both the Sun and our heart perform the same functions. If our aim is to bring our human consciousness into alignment with Divine consciousness, we focus upon the heart because it is magically related to the exalted creative forces of the Solar System in which we live, and its central feature, the Sun, whose stellar nature mediates the spiritual power of beauty, harmony and radiance. The nature of the heart as the Sun within our body makes it the

[16] Gikatilla, Rabbi Joseph. *Gates of Light: The First English Translation of the Classic Introduction to Jewish Mysticism*, HarperCollins publishers, 1994.
[17] Fortune, Dion. *The Mystical Qabalah*, Weiser Books 2000, pg 196.

perfect meeting place for the combined forces of Earth, Heaven, Who We Are and What We Know.

Another metaphysical principle justifying the heart as the most appropriate location for the center of The Sacred Cross was referenced at the beginning of the book, but certainly bears repeating in this context. It is simply this: living within and acting from our heart is a vital part of the simply human to divinely human transformation many of us seek today. Further, the imbalances within in our ecosystems, our schools, our government systems and our business cultures are demanding that we make the transition to heart-centered thinking now. We have lived in a time of intellectually-centered consciousness for far too long. Through the strength of the mind, we have rationalized, justified and otherwise logically manipulated ourselves into difficulties, the likes of which have not been seen before. We have been told again and again by our spiritual teachers that we must make the shift from intellectually-centered living to heart-centered living. Well founded heart-centered tools, like The Sacred Cross, possess the innate ability to guide users away from our habit body's attachment to intellectually-centered living and toward heart-centered living. We don't even have to think about it or effort. If we work with The Sacred Cross, the repetition of this heart-centered meditation will being to soften the over-stimulated intellect that many of us have fostered and awaken the heart consciousness that we crave.

Having touched upon the three rationales for the heart's function as the center of The Sacred Cross, let us enter into a short meditation which will connect you to your own human heart in preparation for your work with the whole form. If you are using the CD companion to this book, go now to track 3.

Heart Meditation

Take a few moments to release all prior occupations and come into a place of mental, physical and emotional stillness.

Focus your will, attention and sacred imagination upon the physical organ of heart that lies beneath your sternum. Sense the living presence of your own heart seated within the embrace of the expansion and contraction of your lungs. Notice the spiritual energy working around and within the physical heart. With your inner senses engaged, quietly observe the gentle beating of your physical heart.

Now reorient your awareness into the whole physical body. Sense the working relationship between the heart and the arteries, veins and blood vessels, organs and tissues within the body. Sense, see and feel the relationship between the heart and whole. Sit in quiet appreciation of this relationship.

While still aware of all that is occurring within your physical body, begin to conjure your sense of the transpersonal heart of creation. Sense the connection of your physical heart with the physical hearts of all people...all creatures...with the rising and falling sap of the plant kingdom. Listen to the compounded sound of the beating of all hearts...the movement of the vital fluids within all living beings. Sense the exchange of spiritual energies between all living creatures. In stillness, commune with the transpersonal heart of creation.

Relax this orientation to the transpersonal heart....coming gently back to where you once again observe your heart in relation to the whole physical body. Softly release this too...allowing your awareness to be guided back to the physical heart as it pumps life into and through itself. Gently and completely, release even this vision as you return your awareness to the outer world of form.

The Earth Arm of The Sacred Cross

The second component of The Sacred Cross is the Earth arm. It is the first extension from our Heart as we invoke The Cross; as such, it grounds and vitalizes the entire form.

The Earth arm of The Sacred Cross connects us to the physical and metaphysical strata that span the downward progression from the surface of the Earth to its inner core. Through our activation of this arm we are able to access the elemental qualities of the surface and subsurface Earth as well as the vital energy that resides within the core of the planet itself. As it is the realm that houses the soils and spirits that provide a foundation for all life on the surface of the planet, its energies are both grounding and invigorating.

When we invoke the Earth arm of The Sacred Cross, we open ourselves to receive (into our physical body system) this vital, grounding energy for ourselves. We do this, not to merely or selfishly support ourselves, but to support ourselves in light of all that we, in turn, support throughout the course of our lives. As men, women, mothers, fathers, partners, workers, students, children, artists, healers, teachers and the like, we exist upon this Earth as souls embodied to experience, receive from and give back to the world of form. Without a relationship to the Earth and its spiritual forces, how can we hope to experience embodiment to the fullest? Further, how can we endeavor to save a planet to which we have no real spiritual relationship? As neither is possible, let us deepen our exploration of the Earth arm and all its potential invites us to embody within ourselves.

In the context of our work with The Sacred Cross, knowledge of the basic composition of the Earth is important. Let me explain why and as I do, please realize that even though this information is being relayed in the context of the Earthly realms, it is true of all other realms to which we relate spiritually.

As men and women of spirit, we are used to using tools such as dreams, visions and meditations as a means to connect to the beings and energies of the otherworlds with whom we wish to commune and partner. As was previously expressed, we do this by extending our consciousness beyond our personal sphere and into the greater spheres of consciousness that house these other forms of consciousness. It is important to note that as we extend our consciousness beyond our sphere and into the other realms, we will encounter the spiritual resonance of *physical places we journey through and to*. For instance, when we expand our consciousness toward the deep Earth, we will encounter the spiritual resonance of the physical trees, crystals, archeological remains and bones that actually exist there. Because we encounter what's actually there, it is helpful if we take the time to acquaint ourselves with the physical nature of the spiritual environments to which we are seeking a connection. When we know the physical nature of the places and things with which we wish to commune spiritually, we gain their metaphysical keys as well.

To begin our exploration of this arm's capacity, let's briefly speak to the composition of the Earth itself, both physically and metaphysically. Physically our planet is composed of several consecutive layers of geological matter from the outer crust on the surface to the inner core some 3-4,000 miles beneath. The outer surface or crust of the Earth consists of giant tectonic plates and deep oceans that provide habitats for the living plants, minerals and creatures that reside within them. The surface layer provides many unique environments (e.g. aqueous and earthen) that sustain various forms of creation. Beneath the surface layer the material density, mobility and temperature of our planet changes and increases.[18] As we permeate the surface crust and journey into the mantle of the Earth, we find many different strata of rock. Nearer the Earth's surface the rocks are cool and brittle; toward the Earth's core the rocks become increasingly soft and hot. As we speak to the physical nature of the Earth's subsurface environment, it is interesting to realize that encased within the various layers of the subsurface Earth are all the physical remnants of all the living beings and civilizations that have come before. Here we find the skeletons, fossils, pottery chards and other remnants of all things past. It is both comforting and stunning to realize that one day, in some form, we too will be a part of the Earth's subterranean imprint.

Beyond the mantle of the Earth we find the outer and inner core of the planet. Through seismic, geological and gravitational analysis, scientists generally understand that the deepest interior of the planet is composed of a solid inner core and a molten outer core. The molten outer core is believed to

---

[18] www.geology.com, Earth's internal structure.

be made of an iron and nickel alloy, while the solid inner core is thought to be composed mostly of iron.

Now that we have refreshed our knowledge of the physical Earth and come to understand its relevance to our work, let's explore its metaphysical nature where the keys to our deeper relationship to the spiritual Earth can be found.

The layers of the metaphysical Earth mirror the layers of the physical Earth. We begin with the surface world of living plants, minerals and creatures. Within each tree, bush, rock or animal, a living spirit exists; and this spirit expresses the primal nature of the being that houses it. If we burrow beyond the surface world and into the subsurface world beneath, we encounter the ancestral, faery and underworld realms. The beings and energies of these realms create and implement the blueprint for the surface world. In the subsurface world we also encounter the living memory of the planet and all forms of intelligence that have dwelled upon or within it. Magically, the realms of the ancestors, faeries and underworld are collectively referred to as the intra-planetary realms. In the Directional/Elemental Model, the intra-planetary realms are referred to as The Below.

As mentioned several times before, our connections to the otherworldly realms offer us insights into and partnerships with the spiritual beings and energies that dwell there. Through the Earth arm of The Sacred Cross, we connect to the primal, creative powers of the deep Earth and are thus able to commune with the ancestral, faery and underworld beings of the intra-planetary realms. To begin we need only focus our attention and sacred imagination upon the physical forms found upon and within the Earth. We can, for instance, conjure the living images of plant, tree, soil, rock, root, cave, crystal or bone. From here we must allow ourselves to open to the spiritual aspects of the same by connecting to the ancestral, faery and underworld beings and energies. Finally, we come to know the planet's innermost core where the elemental power of the living planet, and all realms it houses, resides. It is here, beyond the layers of physical and metaphysical associations that we encounter a particular quality of light and energy known as the "Earthlight." In his book by the same title, R.J. Stewart writes: "If we work with the Light within the Earth, the energy inherent in the underworld within and beneath our conscious interpretation of our environment, remarkable changes occur.[19]" If you are new to the intra-planetary traditions of the deep Earth, I highly recommend you read any (or all) of these three books written by R.J. Stewart: *Earthlight, Power within the Land* and *The Well of Light.* His long devotion to these realms makes his work second to none.

I have come to believe that all human spiritual and magical work must honor and engage the physical and spiritual Earth in some meaningful fashion. In fact, I would go so far as to say that absolutely no spiritual training is truly complete without it. We are humans, embodied upon this glorious Earth, this is our temple. We did not incarnate here to spend all our time working to transcend our Earthly humanity by ascending out of the body. We came here to lovingly, respectfully and sustainably co-create with the beings and energies of the Earth. Though many living human beings choose to forget to pay homage to and commune with the beings and energies of the

---

[19] Stewart, R.J. *Earth Light: The Ancient Path to Transformation Rediscovering the Wisdom of the Celtic and Faery Lore*, Mercury Publishing 1998., pg 68.

deep Earth, men and women of spirit do not. Through physical Earth working (gardening & tending), meditation (consciousness attunement) and offerings (gifts given in reverence such as wine, beer or baked goods), men and women of spirit of all traditions remember *their own,* and seek to restore *our own,* visceral connection to the primal powers of the planet.

As we invoke the Earth arm of The Sacred Cross, we will encounter the cooler crust of the Earth and all the life forms and imprints that it holds. We will meet the mantle beneath the surface and the increasing density, mobility and temperature that it houses. And finally, we will come upon the planetary core where the primal fire, or Earthlight, dwells. In other words, as we journey toward the deep Earth, we will encounter each of its deepening layers. In turn, the living, spiritual intelligence within these layers will meet, affect and demand things of our consciousness.

Now that we have laid the foundation for the Earth-bound arm of The Cross, let us cultivate a meditative experience of the same. If you are using the CD companion to this book, go now to track 5.

Earth Meditation

If your feet do not presently rest upon the floor or ground beneath you, reposition them so that they do.

Take a few moments to release all prior occupations and come into a place of mental, physical and emotional stillness.

Use your will forces, attention and sacred imagination to focus your awareness on the soles of your feet. See, sense and feel them opening physically and energetically to the vital Earth beneath them. Whether you are outside actually touching the Earth or high off the ground in a many storied building, it does not matter, for as long as you are upon this planet, the vital energy of the Earth is available to you. In trust of this knowing, open the soles of your feet to the Earth. Extend your inner senses of smell, taste, touch, hearing and sight to commune with the physical and energetic attributes of the beings and energies that reside within. Use your sacred imagination to visualize yourself traveling downward, through the soles of your feet and into soft Earth. Use your inner senses to court the physical and energetic attributes of the Earth. Smell the warm soil, see all the life within the Earth, taste the salts and deep aquifers, hear the moans of the tree roots permeating the soils, feel the presence of the tectonic giants within the planet itself. Invite them to come close of you...in turn, open to them. Come to know the Earth on your own terms; open to your own visceral knowing of its vital and ancient nature; commune in this awareness. This communion will guide you in the eventual invocation of the Earth arm of The Sacred Cross.

As you linger within the deep Earth, you may be approached by the beings and energies that live within the faery and underworld realms. Do not force or reach for contact, let come what comes without force or coercion. If Earthen beings present themselves, assess your mutual compatibility. Ask questions of these beings such as "Why do you come to me now?" Take note of the answers. If satisfactory, engage with these beings for a short time. If no beings present themselves, simply tend your courtship of the primal and energetic power of the deep Earth.

Now, gently let go of your orientation to the deep Earth. Gently and thoroughly, rise through the smells, sights, sounds, feelings and taste of the subterranean Earth. Aware of the soles of your feet, pull your own extended energies back into your body. When you are totally and completely home, make a conscious decision to seal the soles of your feet, locking into your body this experience of the deep and enduring Earth.

Gently and completely let go of the focus of this meditation and return your awareness to your physical body and the physical world of form.

The Heavens Arm of The Sacred Cross

From here, let us shift the focus of our attention from the depths of the Earth to the heights beyond and the second extension of The Sacred Cross, the Heavens arm. To begin, I will address the use of the term, the Heavens. When referring to the Heavens in our work with The Sacred Cross, we do so without orienting toward the viewpoint of any one religion or spiritual tradition. Instead, the intention is to find common ground among the various spiritual systems.

When we speak of the Earth, its tangibility and commonality in our lives provides for an immediate and clear connection; we all see, touch and live upon the same Earth. Further, we have just established that in a spiritual sense, the term "Earth" refers to the surface and intra-planetary faery, ancestral and underworld realms. For the most part, the spiritual aspects of the Earth share the same common acceptance; most of the traditions that honor the Earth do so through contact with the ancestral, faery or underworld beings and energies to which they personally and collectively relate. Thus in our work with the Earth realm both physically and metaphysically we have some degree of commonality.

When we speak of the Heavens, we do not tend to find the same consistency of understanding. This is partly due to the fact that the physical and metaphysical consideration of this term is not necessarily held in common among spiritual seekers or their systems; the Heavens certainly mean different things to different people. Some hold the Heavens as a physical place that exists far above the Earth, oriented to and yet beyond time. Some believe the Heavens to be not a physical place at all, but instead a condition of consciousness. For others, the Heavens is the place where a supreme being(s) resides surrounded by hosts of angels, archangels and other spiritual beings of the higher dimensions. And yet others hold the Heavens as the sacred Direction of the Above and a place where the starry dancers, future generations or watchful spirits reside. Though these distinctions can and do create several degrees of separation between the various spiritual practices we humans engage in, one point of commonality does prevail. It is here that we find the basis for the definition of the Heavens used in The Sacred Cross.

The point of commonality within the realm of the Heavens is this: the beings and energies that reside there are not fixed within or upon the physical Earth and thus are not bound to our particular world of form. In a word, they are beings and energies that exist "off-planet" and are thus seen as Divine in some fashion. This is the familiar factor among the ways in which the various traditions observe the Heavens. And thus it is here that we find our common ground for using the term.

The names and associations will vary depending upon the tradition you hold as sacred; however, when you work with the Heavens in The Sacred Cross the aim is to attune to the aspect of the off-planet Divine you revere most. For some this is God, Goddess, Great Spirit, Allah or Buddha; for others it is Isis, Sky Father, Love, Peace or their own Higher Self. Each and every one of these beings exists beyond a physical body and off-planet and is thus appropriate to include in our work.

Religions and spiritual traditions are very personal, and people become very personally attached to their understanding of who or what they consider Divine. In my work with The Sacred Cross and in my spiritual practice in general, I have found that as I age and grow I am less and less concerned with the cultural or telesmatic imagery that distinguishes our religious practices and separates us as a spiritual human race. I am instead drawn more and more to a single point of light that exists in the center of our many-spoked Wheel of Life where the various temples, religions, traditions and expressions of the Divine find their roots and their inspiration. Our religions and traditions are important for they are the means through which we come to know our wholeness within and the holiness beyond us. However, at this point in our history, I feel the time has come for our religions to guide us toward the common grace and sacred union of all faiths, where distinction fades and unity prevails. We are, after all, one human family and it is in our unity that we find our strength. As you work with the Heavens in The Sacred Cross form, begin by holding fast to the tradition of your choosing. Then, if you are willing, begin to seek out the flame of unity that burns for all people across all religions and traditions. If you are willing, over time, start to shift the Heavenly orientation of this arm of The Sacred Cross toward the unity flame. In this particular frame of visioning and orientation you will find, as I have, that your abilities and capacities with this tool are greatly amplified.

Now that you have a basic appreciation of what is meant by the Heavens in The Sacred Cross, it is important to claim and strengthen your own felt sense of this realm in meditation. If you are working with the CD, please go to track 6 now.

Heaven Meditation

Come into a comfortable meditative posture, making sure that the top of your head is free of any non-essentials (e.g. baseball cap, headphone wires, hair clips, etc.); if you routinely meditate with items such as a headscarf or prayer veil continue their use for this meditation.

Take a few moments to release all prior occupations and come into a place of mental, physical and emotional stillness.

Direct your will, attention and sacred imagination to focus your awareness on the desire to commune with the spiritual beings and energies of the Heavens. Focusing on the crown at the top of your head, see, sense and feel its natural resonance with the eternal Heavens beyond you. Whether you are inside your home or in a bus traveling home from work, it does not matter for the inspiration of the Heavens is always available to you. In trust of this knowing, open the crown of your head to the Heavens. Use your sacred imagination to assist you by extending your senses through the crown of your head, beyond the sphere of your physical body and into the layers of air and space beyond your physical form.

See yourself gliding through tree branches and into clouds...above the clouds and toward the atmosphere of the Earth itself...beyond this atmosphere and into the vast expanse of the galaxy and Universe beyond. Continue this extension until you find yourself in the presence of the Heavens, home to the expression of the Divine you most revere. Use your inner senses of smell, taste, touch, hearing and sight to commune with the physical and energetic attributes of the beings and energies that reside within. Invite them to come close to you...in turn, open to them. This communion will help you in the eventual invocation of the Heavenly arm of The Sacred Cross.

As you linger here, you may experience a new or different sense of the Divine you revere most. You may also receive an inspirational thought, vision or message. Do not force or reach for contact here, let come what comes without force or coercion. If previously unknown spiritual beings present themselves, assess their presence and your mutual compatibility. Ask questions of these beings such as "Why do you come to me now?" Take note of the answers. If satisfactory, cautiously engage with these beings for a short time. If no beings present themselves, stay in courtship of your awareness of the inspirations and insights of the Heavens.

Now, gently let go of your attunement to the Heavens. Release your attachment to the smells, sights, sounds, feelings and taste of this place. Pull all extended energies back into your body, slowly and deliberately. See yourself back in the galaxy orienting toward the Earth, coming back into the atmosphere of our planet and toward the highest clouds soaring below you...moving through the layers of clouds you near the tallest branches of the trees you soared through previously. See your own physical body below you. Restore the union of your consciousness and your physical body. Seated within the physical body, reorient your bodily awareness back to the crown of your head. Make a conscious decision to seal your crown, locking into your body this experience of the inspirational and insightful Heavens.

Gently and completely release the intention of this meditation and return your awareness to the physical world within which it rests now.

The Element of "Who I Am"

The third extension of The Sacred Cross is the arm of "Who I Am." It harbors the remembered and embodied aspects of our essential and enduring human self. To set the context for this arm, let's explore exactly what is meant by the phrase "essential and enduring human self."

Each one of us comes into this life bearing particular imprints that, more or less, stay with us throughout our incarnation. First, we step into a line of ancestors, thus commanding a surname complete with its own particular cultural and genetic imprinting. It is from this genealogical foundation that we ascertain our physical attributes such as hair, skin and eye color, height, shoe size, etc. We also receive a unique astrological imprint that is composed of the precise arrangement of stars and planets at the moment of our first breath. Through our natal aspects we come to possess certain personality traits, aspirations, tendencies and likely life paths. We also bear or learn (via our reactionary coping mechanisms) particular personality traits, often referred to as our "shadows," which are quite purposeful as well. All of these various elements co-mingle to create what I refer to as our essential self. It is this essential self that comprises the third arm of The Sacred Cross, aptly called "Who I Am" (also referred to as "Who You Are" or "Who We Are"). Knowledge of "Who We Are" is very important to our spiritual and magical work. Though as men and women of spirit, much of what we aim for takes us beyond the realms of the personality, it is important to honor the personality cloak we came in to this life prepared to wear.

If you are uncertain as to the place "Who I Am" holds in your spiritual and magical work, I have these thoughts to share. We live in a world where so many people spend millions of dollars trying to convince us of the virtues of being someone other than ourselves. Each day I turn on my computer, innocently endeavoring to check my e-mails, only to be bombarded by multitudes of blinking advertisements telling me that to be complete my lips should be puffier, my tummy flatter, my skin smoother and my wardrobe should copy the fashion sense of the latest Hollywood honey. Through such advertisements, we are constantly enticed to abandon the discovery of "who we are" and instead *become more like someone else.* After all the work our soul and its otherworldly companions did to prepare for the exactitude of the conception, birth and execution of a human life, it seems blasphemous to endeavor to become someone or something other than our own embodiment of the Divine. For all of the hype justifying imitation as the sincerest form of flattery, Socrates did not advise the young Athenian Alcibiades to heed his good advice by living in accordance with the Delphic inscription "know another." On the contrary,

Socrates told Alcibiades to "know thyself.[20]" Because it is so often misunderstood or misused, a digression explaining the true origins of this much quoted and seldom credited axiom is fitting.

According to my research, the first time the oft-quoted phrase "know thyself" was exhibited in writing was in Plato's *The First Alcibiades*. In that text, the young Alcibiades speaks to Socrates about all he must do to succeed as a military general. He talks specifically of his endeavors to learn the tactical strategies of the generals and armies he must oppose. In response, Socrates tells Alcibiades that knowledge of the self is a far more important occupation. And he expands his point further to say this: to know one's self is to know our true source; without knowing the Divine that is our true source, we cannot know ourselves. An excerpt from this pivotal Socratic teaching follows.

> "Socrates: And is self-knowledge such an easy thing, and was he to be lightly esteemed who inscribed the text on the temple at Delphi? Or is self-knowledge a difficult thing, which few are able to attain?
>
> Alcibiades: At times I fancy, Socrates that anybody can know himself; at other times the task appears to be very difficult.
>
> Socrates: But whether easy or difficult, Alcibiades, still there is no other way; knowing what we are, we shall know how to take care of ourselves, and if we are ignorant we shall not know.[21]"

---

[20] Floyer, Sydenham. The Works of Plato: His Fifty-Five Dialogues and Twelve Epistles, Volume 1, The First Alcidiades, AMS Press, NY 1972.
[21] Jowett, Benjamin, The First Alcibiades. University of Adelaid Library, Adelaid Australia, 2006.

To Socrates, to know thyself was to live life in harmonious awareness of the Creator from whom we come and to whom we will one day return. All are embodied with a mission to gain self-possession which necessarily involves a reunification with our origins both in soul and in essence[22]. Socrates' advice to the young military commander was to spend less of his precious life devoted to the strategies of military service and more time devoted to the discovery of his own Divine nature. Would he not say the same to us today by perhaps advising us to spend less time surfing internet gossip, watching reality television and betting on sporting events? Would Socrates not tell us that spending time contemplating our humanity as an emanation of the Divine expression would be a far better use of our free time? In our work with The Sacred Cross, we find that knowledge of the self, as both a decidedly human entity and an expression of the Divine, is paramount. This resolutely stated, let us spend a few moments addressing our essential self, both in "light" and in "shadow."

I have long believed that we cannot excel spiritually in this life if we are constantly trying to avoid seeing and accepting the totality of our human virtues and vices. To become fully embodied as men and women of spirit, we must accept the glorious abilities and that we possess, and through which a certain quality of light enters the world. We must also accept the shattered, cluttered and tainted aspects we've also accumulated. For some, the acceptance of the light is the greatest challenge, for others it is the acceptance of the shadow that perplexes them most. Because the "Who I Am" arm is the dwelling place for both our "shadow" and our "light," as you

---

[22] O'Daly, Gerard J.P. Plotinus' Philosophy of Self, Irish University Press, Shannon Ireland, 1973.

begin your work with it you may feel the tension or polarity between these divergent personal aspects. In this, the friction or dissonance between your lighter and shadowy sides may feel heightened as you begin your work with The Cross. While this may feel challenging initially, stick with the process. The harmonizing of the initial polarities of the Earth and Heaven arm discussed previously applies here as well. Thus, over time this tension will soften and the two "sides" of your nature will harmonize. The amalgamation of our coarser nature into our clearer nature is one of the unique gifts The Sacred Cross offers its users. And as is the case with most energy medicine, the symptoms can feel worse before they (and we) feel better.

Once you begin to experience the weave between your shadowy and light-filled elements, you will catalyze the process of incorporating your Personality and your Individuality; the specifics of this amalgamation are described in the chapter on the esoteric aspects of The Sacred Cross. With this incorporation comes an increase in the acuity of our spiritual senses that alleviates the light/shadow tension altogether, elevating the Personality into the Individuality. The gains fostered by this alleviation and elevation are well worth the initial discomfort we may experience.

With the intellectual specifics of the "Who I Am" arm of The Sacred Cross in place, it is again time to turn our attention to a visceral experience of the same. Written below is a meditative journey called *The Mirror of Sun and Moon*. *The Mirror of Sun and Moon* is a visionary oracle found within the collective inner realms. To those who seek with a sincere mind and an open heart, this oracle offers an unadulterated reflection of both our exterior and interior self. In an external sense, *The Mirror of Sun and Moon* reflects to us the physical attributes of our ancestors of blood and the lineage we carry. It shows us who we are as seen by others in a positive and inspiring manner. It also reflects any disharmony within our nature that is seen by others who look upon us or interact with us day by day. In an internal sense, *The Mirror of Sun and Moon* reflects the emotional and spiritual patterns of our primal inner nature. It burrows beneath the surface, excavating the energetic forms, belief systems and modes of thinking of the internal self that eventually inform the external self.

As a spiritual and magical oracle, *The Mirror of Sun and Moon* is accessible by anyone that has eyes to see and a heart to hear the truth of who they are, in reflection. Be mindful that this meditation tool is not truly accessible to those who only wish to possess a fortification of and justification for their own spiritual stagnation and human complacency. Thus, endeavor to remain open, soft and willing to receive the reflections that this great mirror offers you in love and compassion. If you are working with the CD, please listen to track 8 now.

Mirror of Sun and Moon Meditation

With a clear intention in your heart and mind, let us journey to the Mirror of Sun and Moon. Releasing all prior occupations, come into a place of stillness.

Using your sacred imagination, see yourself in a quiet and formless place, where the distinguishments of neither day nor night can be found. Allow this vast stillness to comfortably envelop you completely.

In this stillness, gently recall your intention to meet The Mirror of Sun and Moon. In this, be clear that you possess openness of mind and sincerity of heart. As this intention settles around and within you, you begin to sense a stirring within the Earth beneath your feet. Spiraling out of the Earth before you are two metal staffs, one is silver and the other gold. Watch as the gold and silver staffs twist and turn in an upward motion until they reach the exact height of your physical body. From the top of the silver spiraling staff, an icon of the glistening full Moon forms. From the top of the gold spiraling staff, an icon of the radiant Sun forms.

In the space between the gold and silver staffs you see an emergence of random flashes of reflective light. Slowly these twinkling reflections grow and solidify into a large oval mirror suspended in the space between the two staffs. Notice how the gold of the Sun staff and the silver of the Moon staff wind around the luminous mirror in a powerful and purposeful embrace. You are standing before the Mirror of Sun and Moon. This mirror possesses the ability to reflect that which others see when they look upon you, as well as the hidden aspects of yourself that lie within you. Your intention is to see the reflections that assist you to create the "Who I Am" arm of The Sacred Cross. With this intention, coupled with a willingness to see, look upon yourself within the Mirror.

When you are ready to receive a clear sense of the gifts and challenges you offer outwardly to the world, gently lift your hand to touch the icon of the Sun. As you do, watch the reflection change before you. Spend time witnessing the many personal reflections that offer themselves to you now. See each and every aspect of your external self as viewed from outside. See both light and shadow here.

When you know the Sun's offering from the Mirror is complete for now, give thanks and touch the icon atop the staff of spiraling gold. Wait in stillness for several moments.

When you are ready to receive a clear sense of the gifts and challenges living within you, gently lift your hand to touch the icon of the Moon. As you do, watch the reflection change before you as image after image presents itself to you. Spend time witnessing the many reflections that offer themselves to you now. See each and every aspect of your internal self, both that which is clearly known and that which is lesser known within you. See both light and shadow in the mirror's reflection. When you know the offering from the Moon is complete for now, give thanks and touch the icon atop the staff of spiraling silver. Wait in stillness for several moments.

Complete, for now, watch as the Mirror of Sun and Moon begins to slowly dissolve and the staves of Sun and Moon recede into the quiet Earth. Now gently and completely release the intention of this meditation and return your awareness to the physical world and your waking consciousness.

The Element of "What I Know"

In addition to the prescribed personal characteristics we come into this life bearing, we also acquire or gather knowledge and skills that sculpt the man or woman of spirit that we will become. With this thought in mind, it is time to turn our attention to the fourth and final arm of The Sacred Cross, for it is within its embrace that the repository of our life's work is held. Here we find the compendium of the skills, tools and living knowledge we've acquired; thus we call this arm "What I Know" (also referred to as "What You Know" or "What We Know.")

Some people are initially perplexed as to why their occupations or avocations hold a place of prominence in The Sacred Cross. Many of us seek refuge in our spiritual and magical work as a means of escaping the pressures of our work-a-day lives. Why, then, do we include this aspect of ourselves in this work? The answer to this question is really quite simple. Contrary to the popularized spiritual opinions of some, there really is no dividing line between our "personal" self and our "spiritual" self. We are one being, and all we do impacts the physical body, consciousness and soul that we are.

For whatever reasons, many of us compartmentalize ourselves and our lives into "mundane" and "spiritual" categories. I do not agree with this approach. Our soul does not only grow or stagnate within the bounds of our *spiritual* contemplations and actions; it grows or stagnates within the bounds of the whole of our lives. Everything we experience while embodied, from our jobs, parenting activities and eating choices to our web surfing habits and hairstyle, provides an opportunity for the expression of our soul's purpose. As such, these aspects are included in the wholeness of "What We Know."

Within the "What I Know" arm, there are two slightly different expressions. Let me take a moment to explain what they are. In an initial sense, the skills, tools and knowledge we've acquired make us craftsmen and craftswomen of a life, for they shape and change who we become. All our choices, ranging from vocation to avocation, merge together in a way that sets the course for the specific manner in which we unfold. The skills and knowledge we acquire become the means through which we employ the raw materials of "Who We Are". This employment creates the expression of our life's work. In other words, our nature or "Who We Are" creates the interest and enthusiasm to learn and gather "What We Know."

The "What We Know" arm of The Sacred Cross actualizes our soul's yearning; it is the means through which we express "Who We Are." The "What I Know" arm of The Cross also provides the link between our purely personal expression and our relational offering to the whole. It is through our skills, tools and knowledge that we touch others, giving of ourselves to our families, communities and the world. When we work within the Directional/Elemental Model described later, we will find that it is the "What I Know" arm that opens the way for the transition between ourselves and the primal world of nature. It is because this arm takes us outward, into our relationships with the world, that we invoke it last.

When we begin our work as men and women of spirit, our initial task is to melt the boundaries of perception that keep our consciousness locked into the physical or seen world. On the other side of these melted perceptions is the remembrance of our interconnectedness with the spiritual worlds and the primal world of nature. Once we remember our interconnection, it is much easier to know and understand the sacred service we can offer to the greater wholeness we serve. In our initial efforts toward this shift in perception, the "What I Know" arm is especially helpful. It assists us to let go of any arbitrary compartmentalization of our mundane and spiritual lives and instead live every aspect of our lives as if we are being witnessed by the spiritual elders whom we revere as most holy, because in fact, from the soul's perspective, we are. Once we've addressed the truly arbitrary splits between our perceptions of the "sacred" versus the "mundane" within ourselves, we are in a better position to heal any splits that manifest in our perceptions of the seen and unseen worlds. In other words, until we melt the boundaries erected between our own "sacred" and "mundane" self, we cannot melt the boundaries which unify the mundane/seen and sacred/unseen worlds within which we live; one shift in perception begets the other. Thus, it is important to include "What We Know" into our spiritual and magical work.

In the formation of the prior three arms of The Sacred Cross, our culminating exploration occurred in meditation. In the formation of the "What I Know" arm, we contemplate this question instead: "What skills, tools and knowledge have I acquired throughout my life that I give in service to myself and others?" When you answer this question think broadly, recalling all you know or have learned. In your list of skills, tools and knowledge, include the work you've done as friend, mother, father, poet, athlete, gardener and listener, along with the perhaps more obvious work as accountant, teacher, lawyer, therapist, artist and writer. Look for any overarching themes that present themselves within your life's achievements. Once you have completed your entire list describing "What I Know," organize the list into the overarching themes of your life's work. See if you can determine the three to five skill sets that you feel represent the greater motifs of your life's work thus far. These motifs will serve as the foundation of your "What I Know" arm henceforward.

Having touched upon all five components of The Sacred Cross in their foundational sense, we are now ready to progress toward our invocation of each element (Heart, Earth, Heaven, "Who I Am," "What I Know") within the context of the wholeness they co-create. Before stepping into that experience, you may find it helpful to contemplate your answers to the questions that conclude Part 2, as a clear sense of your relationship to each of these five components will greatly enhance your initial work with The Sacred Cross in its entirety.

Part 2: Questions & Contemplations

In this section we focused on building an intellectual and experiential connection to each of the five components of The Sacred Cross: Heart, Earth, Heaven, "Who I Am" and "What I Know." Before moving on to the invocation forms for The Sacred Cross, take the time to capture and record the fruits of your explorations in relationship to these five components: Heart, Earth, Heavens, "Who I Am" and "What I Know."

1. What aspects of the Heart meditation were most alive and vital for you?

2. What presented itself to you most clearly with regard to the Earth meditation? Reiterate what you remember of this meditation and all you sensed within it.

3. When you experienced the Heavens meditation how did this realm present itself to you? Did anything change with regard to your knowing of the Divine?

4. In your meditation with *The Mirror of Sun and Moon* what did you experience with regard to your external reflection as viewed by others? Likewise, what did you experience with regard to your internal self, known and unknown?

5. What broad themes or motifs did you discover in relationship to your skills and tools in the "What I Know" arm contemplation?

Part 3: Practical Applications

Construction of The Sacred Cross: Introduction

There are two basic methods for invoking The Sacred Cross, The Long Form and The Short Form. Both are important in the overall use of The Cross.

The Long Form provides us with a thorough, step-by-step approach which enables us to build a deep relationship to each arm, the whole and the realms within and beyond us. The Long Form's slow, methodical invocation offers particular meditative insights that come from an intentional interaction with each of the layers of perception we move through using this form (e.g. each part of the body, each layer of the tunneling Earth, etc.). The Long Form also helps us cultivate meditative concentration and endurance.

The Short Form's concise construction teaches us how to invoke The Cross quickly and reliably in under one minute. Thus it grants us the agility of a focused, instantaneous connection that helps to recondition our mind away from knee-jerk reactions that rise up within us when we are suddenly faced with an immediate personal challenge or need. In this way, The Short Form helps us to retrain our automatic habit-body responses, moving us away from reaction and toward right action in any given situation.

There is no need to completely master The Long Form before you begin to experiment with The Short Form. To achieve the best results, work with the Long and Short Form in rotation. The forms utilize different spiritual muscles; thus one form strengthens the other. To begin, we will work with The Long

Form as its slow and methodical approach will benefit the new user. In the section that follows, The Short Form will be introduced. As you prepare to invoke the Long and Short Forms, take a moment to recall all that has been presented to you as a description of the elemental and spiritual power encased within each of the five components of The Sacred Cross. Look back over your answers to the questions at the end of Parts 1 and 2. Refresh yourself with the specifics of your own connections to Earth, Heaven, "Who You Are" and "What You Know" that came through the meditations and reflective contemplations you've performed. When you are ready to proceed with your first invocation, either follow the mediation written below or listen to track 9 of the CD.

Releasing all prior occupations, come into a place of stillness...rest here for several moments.

Begin by orienting your will, attention and sacred imagination upon and within your heart. Allow the gathering of these forces to enliven the light that dwells within your heart. Now, focus these same forces upon the intention of meeting and communing with the beings and energies of the deep Earth.

See the emanation of your heart's light gathering within. Allow this light to pass beyond the heart and into your stomach, hips, legs, knees, calves and feet until the entire lower half of your body is filled with your heart's light. Open the soles of your feet, allowing this light to leave your sphere and permeate the actual physical Earth beneath you. See, sense and feel it burrowing through each and every layer of the Earth beneath your feet. Observe as it courses through the substrata, weaving through tree roots, around granite boulders, through underground aquifers and the remains of civilizations past. As you continue expanding downward, notice that the environment around you becomes warmer, less solid and more molten...and then solid again until at last you find yourself within the central heart fire of the Earth itself. In a loving gesture, offer the light of your heart to the Earth's core; feel its acceptance. See, sense and feel the light and heart fire of your body directly connected to the light and heart fire of the sacred Earth.

Where your heart light was burrowing toward the Earth's center before, the time has come to shift its orientation from expansion to contraction. Prepare to receive its vitality and creativity. As you inhale, slowly and carefully gather and pull this creative vitality upward through all the layers you burrowed through before until you reach your sphere and the soles of your own feet. Open the lower body from toe to heart, to receive the Earth's creative and vital forces.

Allow the exchange to continue between your own heart fire and the creative and vital heart fire within the core of the Earth. This is what it means to be in communion. As you commune with the deep Earth, consciously ground yourself into its protective stability. The first arm of The Sacred Cross is complete. From here, keep one quarter of your awareness moving between the heart fires of yourself and the Earth.

Become aware again of the forces of beauty, harmony and stability within your heart. Engage your sacred imagination, will and attention toward meeting the power and presence of the Heavens. Again sense the light that dwells within your heart; allow this light to move upward. Fill your arms and hands, your throat, and skull until your whole upper body is filled with your heart's light. Open your crown, and allow this light to expand beyond your sphere through and beyond all that is above you. See, sense and feel it soaring past tall tree branches through clouds and out of the atmosphere of the planet itself, into the vast galaxy that lies beyond. Continue this expansive, outward journey beyond the world of form until you reach the world of the formless. In this place of origination, see, sense and feel the spiritual fire that lies within the heart of the Heavenly Divine you most revere. Merge the fire of your own heart with the fire of the spiritual heart of the Divine.

In a loving gesture, offer the light of your heart to the spiritual fire of the high Heavens; feel its acceptance. Where this light within was climbing before, prepare now to shift its orientation from expansion to contraction. Prepare to receive the inspiration and guidance of its spiritual fire. As you inhale, slowly and carefully gather and pull the inspiration and guidance from the Heavens downward through all the layers you climbed through before until you reach your sphere and the crown of your head. Open the upper body from head to heart, to receive the inspiration and guidance of the Heavens.

Allow the exchange to continue between your own heart consciousness and the spiritual heart fire within the Heavens, home of the Divine you revere most. This is what it means to be in communion. As you commune with the high Heavens, consciously uplift yourself into its exalted nature. The second arm of The Sacred Cross is complete; keep another quarter of your awareness upon the exchange between Heaven and heart within you.

Now that both of the vertical arms are established, allow yourself to sit within the "tension" of these two poles. Next, open the entire vertical form so that the essence of your Heavenly and Earthly connections flows throughout the entire body simultaneously. Here the apparent tension between Earth and Heaven meeting in the heart resolves into a harmony that informs your body consciousness. Heavenly inspiration drops into the feet and Earthly grounding extends into the head. Keep half of your conscious awareness seeded within the vertical arms' inflow and outflow between the fires of Heaven and Earth, and return the remaining half of your awareness back to the heart.

Aware of the work occurring with the first two arms of The Sacred Cross, direct your will, attention and sacred imagination to the intention of meeting your unique self. Contract deep within yourself as you call to mind and invoke the presence of your personal attributes and characteristics... your light and your shadow. Shifting from contraction to expansion, invite these aspects of you to come fully alive within you, filling one horizontal arm (either right or left, according to choice) of your Sacred Cross. Let aspects of "Who You Are" be fully awakened from within you and offered outward into and beyond your sphere.

Become aware of the affinity between "Who You Are" and the deep Earth and high Heavens swirling within you. Allow all of "Who You Are" to co-mingle with the supportive inspiration of the Heavens and the Earth. Place the third quarter of your awareness within the motion of third arm of The Cross as you return the final quarter of your awareness back to the heart.

Direct your will, attention and sacred imagination toward the skills, tools and knowledge acquired within your life thus far. Go deep within yourself calling to mind the skills, tools and knowledge you possess. Invoke their full presence...and then expand from within, fully enlivening "What You Know" from the center of your heart's fire outward along the second horizontal arm of your Sacred Cross.

Consciously aware of their mutual affinity, witness the merging of "What You Know", "Who You Are", the deep Earth and the high Heavens. As the vertical and horizontal arms continually expand and contract from the heart, giving and receiving...see how The Sacred Cross becomes four elongated spheres circulating energy and consciousness between Earth, Heaven, "Who You Are" and "What You Know." Return your awareness to the heart, where these four forces meet; commune in this place in stillness, receiving the visions, inspirations and sensations that come. Simply receive the totality of your Sacred Cross.

When this stillness and receptivity is complete, beginning with the fourth arm, "What You Know," release and recoil this arm into the quiet repose of heart. Focusing on the third arm, "Who You Are," release and recoil this arm into the quiet repose of the heart. Now release the upward extension of the second arm of the Heavens allowing it to come to rest within the heart. And finally, release the downward extension of the first arm of the Earth, let it too come to rest within the repose of the heart. Take a few breaths to reorient your awareness to the outer world of form. Return fully to your waking awareness.

Congratulations, you have just completed your first invocation of The Sacred Cross using The Long Form. Before moving on, take a few moments to notice what's different within your physical body system. Write any noticeable shifts, new information or personal reflections on the blank page that follows. When complete, take a break from your Sacred Cross work for at least twenty-four hours. This initial resting period allows your physical body system to integrate its first invocation of The Sacred Cross through a period of rest and repose. As men and women of spirit often attest, it is within the grace of rest and repose that some of our greatest insights manifest.

Personal Reflections upon Completing My First Invocation of The Sacred Cross using The Long Form

Construction of The Sacred Cross: The Short Form

Now that you have experienced The Long Form invocation, you are ready to experience The Short Form. The familiarity gained from the slow and deliberate visualization used in The Long Form creates the pathway for the quicker invocation of The Short Form. Remember, it is recommended that you work with these two forms in rotation. Just as an athlete trains for both speed and endurance, the practitioner of The Sacred Cross should be comfortable working with both the Long and Short Forms.

The Short Form relies upon the partnership of focused attention and breath. To invoke The Sacred Cross using The Short Form, we engage the power of an acutely focused sacred imagination with the calming effect of eight deliberate breathing cycles. As it is a precise working of the sacred imagination and eight breathing cycles, The Short Form requires some practice to master. However, once you've integrated its particular rhythm; your ability to quickly and thoroughly invoke The Sacred Cross will become quite strong. To help you adjust to the precision of The Short Form, each of the eight cycles is clearly referenced in the written version of the meditation that follows this introduction. The method used on the companion CD assumes your familiarity with the eight breathing cycles; as such it does not contain the breathing cycle detail found in the written version. To learn the rhythm of The Short Form, it is important to practice this mediation using the written form before proceeding to the recorded guidance. With this in mind, let's progress to The Short Form; you will find the guided meditation on track 10 of the CD.

Releasing all prior occupations, come into a place of stillness...rest here for several moments. Center your awareness in your heart, sensing the force of beauty, harmony and stability that resides within it.

[Cycle 1] Draw in the power of your breath, while at the same time focusing your intention on uniting with the heart fire of the deep Earth. Slowly and deliberately release the breath while your sacred imagination bores toward the heart fire of the Earth. Once your breath is fully exhausted, hold it while the visualization of your sacred imagination continues onward until it reaches the sacred fire of the deep Earth. This should last another 5-15 seconds. [Cycle 2] Upon the liberation of your next inhale, deliberately pull toward you the flow of energy and power of the deep Earth. Exhale.

[Cycle 3] Draw in the power of your breath, while at the same time focusing your intention on uniting with the heart fire of the high Heavens. Slowly and deliberately release the breath while your sacred imagination climbs toward the heart fire of the Heavens. Once your breath is fully exhausted, hold it while the visualization of your sacred imagination continues onward until it reaches the sacred fire of the Divine you revere most. This should last another 5-15 seconds. [Cycle 4] Upon the liberation of your next inhale, deliberately pull toward you the flow of energy and power of the high Heavens. Exhale.

[Cycle 5] Inhale and exhale, opening the form, and clearly feel yourself centered within Earth's stable grounding and Heaven's inspiring guidance throughout your body.

[Cycle 6] On an inhale, go inward to touch the essence of "Who You Are." On the exhale gift this essence outward along one horizontal arm, filling your personal sphere.

[Cycle 7] On an inhale, go inward to touch the essence of "What You Know." On the exhale gift this essence outward along one horizontal arm, filling your personal sphere.

[Cycle 8] Inhale and exhale as you open the form to co-mingle the horizontal and vertical arms meeting in your heart.

Breathing freely and fully, spend several minutes in the totality of The Sacred Cross; see, sense and feel all that is catalyzed within you and all that is newly available through you.

When this stillness and receptivity is complete, beginning with the fourth arm, "What You Know" release this into the quiet repose of heart. Release the third arm, "Who You Are" into the quiet repose of the heart. Now release the upward extension of the second arm of the Heavens allowing it to come to rest within the heart. And finally, release the downward extension of the first arm of the Earth, letting it too come to rest within the repose of the heart. Take a few breaths to reorient your awareness to the outer world of form. Come fully into your waking awareness.

With the completion of The Short Form, take a few moments to notice what's different within your physical body system. Write any noticeable shifts, new information or personal reflections on the blank page that follows. Notice also the difference between The Long Form and The Short Form. When complete, take a break from your Sacred Cross work for another twenty-four hours, offering yourself the grace of rest and repose while granting any additional insights the space to manifest.

Personal Reflections upon Completing My First Invocation of The Sacred Cross using The Short Form

With this, you have now experienced the two basic forms for invoking The Sacred Cross. Invoke The Long Form or The Short Form, in rotation, each day until you feel you have thoroughly integrated their sequences and their nuances.

Now that we are becoming familiar with the Long and Short Forms of The Sacred Cross on a personal level, it is time to turn our attention toward partnership and our transpersonal work with The Cross. This is done by incorporating The Sacred Cross with the Directional/Elemental Model used in the Western Mysteries Tradition. Though either form may be used for this work (Long or Short), I will use a modified version of The Long Form as it highlights the interface between the two spiritual/magical systems.

The Directional/Elemental Model and The Sacred Cross

The Directional/Elemental Model complements and accentuates the power and purpose of The Sacred Cross. To understand why this is so, let's explore the basis of the Directional/Elemental Model. From there we will discuss the way in which these two systems work in tandem.

The Directions known as North, South, East and West are more than points on a compass; they comprise the foundational orientations that humans have to space, themselves and the planet itself. Likewise the Elements known as Earth, Fire, Air and Water are exceedingly important for they are the physical and magical components of the entire created world. Without the Elements we would not physically exist; and without the Directions we would not have a sense of ourselves in relationship to the world in which we live.

Because the Directions orient us to ourselves, homes, lands and planet, and the Elements comprise every living thing, both have long been considered sacred by those who revere Nature, and its creator, as a primal spiritual power. Men and women who hold Nature in reverence seek to perform our spiritual and magical work under the guidance and protection of the Directions/Elements, while inviting the witness and blessing of the beings and energies that possess an affinity for their purity.

Depending upon the way in which a people's land is oriented and thus their spiritual/magical system is fashioned, each Direction is associated with an Element. In our work with The Sacred Cross we use the spiritual system of the Western Mystery Tradition as it is the system upon which our temple, The StarHouse, was founded. Thus, the Direction North finds its complement in the Element of Earth, the Direction South to the Element of Fire, East to Air and West to Water. The origins of this pairing within the Western Mysteries Model is based upon the people's lands of our Western European ancestors. For them, the Ocean was to the West, the hotter climates to the South, the cooler climates to the North and the long expanse of land to the East. In our magical work today, we honor these same Directional/Elemental associations.

In addition to keeping the Elemental and Directional associations just described, we also recognize the off-planet Direction of Above and its corresponding Elements, the Ethers and Cosmos, and the in-planet Direction of Below and its corresponding Elements, Mineral and Memory. In doing this we recognize the starry and planetary realms that constantly hover beyond us as well as the deep Earthen realms that hold the primal blueprint and ancient memory of the planet itself.

When we seek to affirm our connection to, and thus garner the witness and blessing of, the Directions and Elements, we do so by performing what is called "casting the circle." Because this term is potentially misleading (if the term "circle" is taken too literally), it is worth an explanation as well. When we "cast the circle" composed of North/Earth, South/Fire, East/Air, West/Water, Above/Ethers & Cosmos and Below/Mineral & Memory, we actually create a sphere. As you know, a circle is a two dimensional figure and a sphere is a three dimensional figure. Since we live in three dimensions and not upon a flat diagram, we perform our spiritual and magical work within a sphere.

Beginning with the center, we affirm our relationship to the planetary Directions/Elements of East/Air, South/Fire, West/Water, North/Earth. This creates the four quarters of the sphere in a manner resembling the segments of an orange, in that the directional energy populates a slice of the sphere that extends upward and downward where it meets the other directional segments. Thus, there are high, middle and low aspects to all four quadrants as is illustrated below using the Directions East and West as our example (North and South seen as before and behind the sphere would also follow suit.)

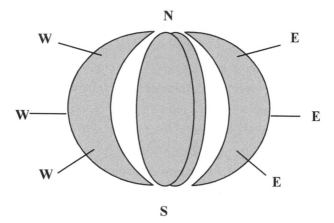

From here, we "crown and found" our field of working by reaffirming our relationship to the Above (A) and Below (B) respectively. This creates a complete sphere about us as illustrated next.

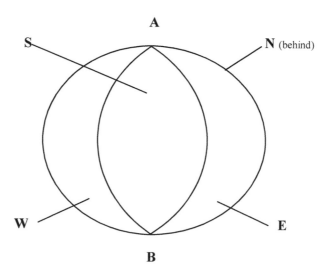

Once we have cast our sphere, we begin to sense the presence of a greater sphere that is composed of and fed by the powers of the Directions and Elements. This greater sphere encompasses or surrounds our personal (or group's) sphere, functioning in two concurrent ways. First, it serves as the working containment for our spiritual and magical practices. Second, it is the portal or filter through which particular spiritual beings and energies may enter into and thus join us within our field of working.

Now that we clearly understand how the Directional/Elemental Model functions on its own, let's discuss how it works in partnership with The Sacred Cross. First, take a moment to notice that Above/Heavens and Below/Earth are common to both systems. In The Sacred Cross, we connect to the Divine through the high Heavens, in the Directional/Elemental Model we open to receive the Cosmos and Ethers in the Above. In the Sacred Cross we connect to the planet's primal creative power through the deep Earth. In the Directional/ Elemental Model we open to receive the Minerals and Memory in the Below. The Ethers, Cosmos and high Heavens are of the same essence. Likewise, the Minerals, Memory and deep Earth are of the same essence. Thus, it is within the Above/Heavens and Below/Earth that we experience the initial confluence of the two systems. The Sacred Cross with its vertical arms extending upwards and downwards mirrors the Directional/Elemental Model's upward extension of the Above and downward extension of Below. Thus the same vertical axis exists within both systems.

From here, the quarterly Directions of North, East, South and West complete a larger sphere. And the two arms "Who I Am" and "What I Know" form the smaller sphere inside it. The illustration that follows should help to solidify your understanding of how these two systems cooperate.

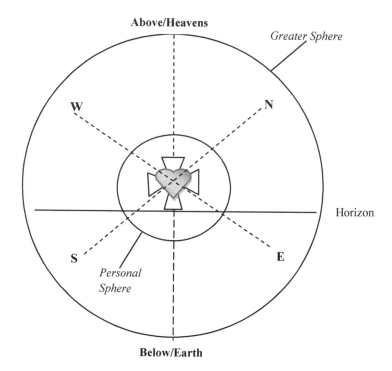

There is an important function served by the incorporation of The Sacred Cross and the Directional/Elemental Model. This function is the easing of the tension that often exists between the dual roles we seek to balance in our lives. In this, I am speaking specifically to the duality between our role as an individual and our role as a member of a greater society. Inherent within this duality is the desire to balance all that we must understand and do to serve ourselves, and all that we must understand and do to serve the greater global family of all living beings of which we are a part.

As men and women of spirit we know that part of our spiritual, magical, an indeed human work, must be performed on our own. This is because much of what we are here to learn, shift, change and augment within ourselves must be accomplished at the personal level. No one can perform the good and the hard work of our simply human to divinely human transformation but us. However, we never perform any work we endeavor to accomplish in a vacuum of the self. We are always operating within the greater whole of which we are an integral part. No matter where we live, we are part of a society, be it sociopolitical, ecological, genealogical or spiritual/primal (that is to say a community, an ecosystem, a family network or the unseen worlds.) Often in our lives we operate within all four societies at once. Thus, in truth, we are both a single human being and part of a living and growing society of many beings, each affecting the other in the greater dance of life, death and regeneration. So though we are responsible for our individual transformational work, this always occurs within and thus affects the societies to which we belong.

As a sacred pattern or system, the circular flow of the Zodiac lays a map before us that offers us additional insights into the cyclic interplay of the polarity between our personal and relational selves. At the beginning of the Zodiac, we awaken into Aries. From here we move through the largely personal expressions of Taurus, Gemini, Cancer and Leo before beginning to assess the fruits of our personal self in Virgo. After that, we come to Libra which awakens us to "other." From here we are sculpted by and through our relationship to the greater society through the signs of Scorpio, Sagittarius, Capricorn and Aquarius until once again, under the influence of Pisces, we are drawn back toward an awareness of our self[23]. Mystical systems like the Zodiac have been formulated over many centuries. They present to us various patterns and possibilities along the pathways we traverse between our simple humanity and our Divine humanity. If we look to these mystical systems (e.g. Zodiac, Qabalah, Tarot and the like), we find that, far from the riddles they initially seem to be, they are instead living matrices full of beings and energies that assist us in our pursuit of enlightenment or unity consciousness.

When we work with The Sacred Cross on an individual basis, we perform part of the work we came here to accomplish as a soul embodied. When we combine The Sacred Cross and the Directional/Elemental Model, and thus place ourselves in communion with the other creative elements and influences within our societies, we perform the relational we work also set before us in this life. As we seek to balance our personal work and our relational work, The Sacred Cross is a wonderful personal tool. When we know we need to focus on our personal spiritual work, we can invoke The Sacred Cross in the self-focused manner highlighted previously. In turn, when we feel our relational spiritual work needs attention, we can invoke The Cross within the Directions/Elements Model. The following meditative method combines the Directional/Elemental Model and The Sacred Cross using a modified version of The Long Form. If you are using the CD, go now to track 12.

---

[23] Rudhyar, Dane. The Pulse of Life: New Dynamics in Astrology, Shambala, 1970.

Releasing all prior occupations, come into a place of stillness...rest here for several moments.

Claim and center your awareness in relationship to where you are physically located now. Affirm your relationship to Below (in-planet) and Above (off- planet). Know where East, South, West and North are in relationship to your physical body.

Now, take your awareness totally and completely into your own heart. Sense the forces of beauty, harmony and stability that reside within it. Clearly envision the glow of your own heart fire. Focus your will, attention and sacred imagination upon uniting your heart fire with the heart fire in the center of the Earth. Visualize these two sacred fires and unite them. Offer the love in your heart fire to the Earth fire. Open yourself to receive the vitality of the Earth fire. Pull this fire toward you, through all the layers below you. Allow it to permeate your entire lower body until you feel heavy with the grounded vitality of the deep Earth. Anchor one quarter of your awareness here in a gesture of giving and receiving.

Return now the fire of your own heart. Clearly envision the glow of your own heart fire. Focus your will, attention and sacred imagination upon the uniting with the Divine heart fire of the Heavens. Visualize these two sacred fires and unite them. Offer the love in your heart fire to the Divine fire. Open yourself to receive the quickening of the Divine fire. Draw down the heart fire of the Heavens toward your heart fire. Allow it to permeate your entire upper body until you feel uplifted with the clear inspiration of the high Heavens. Anchor one quarter of your awareness here in a gesture of giving and receiving.

Now co-mingle the forces of the three fires of heart, Earth and Heaven within your entire body in a continuous line of light and energy traveling from the deep Earth, through your body, to the high Heavens.

Return your awareness to the heart. Direct your will, attention and sacred imagination into your heart's light and power while invoking the inner knowing and presence of "Who You Are." Invite these aspects of you to come fully alive within your inner world...in an outward gesture of expansion, let them flow freely into your personal sphere. Allow all of who you are to be fully present in your heart, body and mind. Anchor one quarter of your awareness here.

Return your awareness to the heart. Direct your will, attention and sacred imagination into your heart's light and power while invoking the inner knowledge and skills that co-create "What You Know." Invite these aspects of you to come fully alive within your inner world.... in an outward gesture of expansion, let them flow freely into your personal sphere. Allow all of what you know to be fully present in your heart, body and mind. Anchor one quarter of your awareness here.

Spend a few moments in the "tension" between the poles of Heaven and Earth. Then, open the form, allowing the vertical arms to unite and co-mingle with the horizontal arms and the harmony within the tension to be realized. Be with the form and force of your Sacred Cross in stillness.

From here, reach outward to the physical East through the winds and breezes you know...moving beyond the physical world, reach to the deities of East who mediate inspiration...moving beyond the mythic, reach toward the essential presence of the eternal East and the power of Life. As you do this, see, sense and feel the energy within your Sacred Cross extending outward into the essence and presence of East. Commune with this elemental power through your Sacred Cross. Feel and sense the way in which the physical, spiritual and essential realms of East impact and inform you.

Now reach outward to the physical South through the warmth and heat you know...moving beyond the physical world, reach to the deities of South who meditate transformation...moving beyond the mythic, reach toward the essential presence of the eternal South and the power of Light. As you do this, see, sense and feel the energy within your Sacred Cross extending outward into the essence and presence of South. Commune with this elemental power through your Sacred Cross. Feel and sense the way in which the physical, spiritual and essential realms of South impact and inform you.

Reach again toward the physical West through the rains and oceans you know...moving beyond the physical world, reach to the deities of West who mediate compassion...moving beyond the mythic, reach toward the essential presence of the eternal West and the power of Love. As you do this, see, sense and feel the energy within your Sacred Cross extending outward into the essence and presence of West. Commune with this elemental power through your Sacred Cross. Feel and sense the way in which the physical, spiritual and essential realms of West impact and inform you.

Reach again toward the physical North through the plants and soils you know...moving beyond the physical world, reach to the deities of North who mediate destruction and regeneration...moving beyond the mythic, reach toward the essential presence of the eternal North and the power of Cosmic Law. As you do this, see, sense and feel the energy within your Sacred Cross extending outward into the essence and presence of North. Commune with this elemental power through your Sacred Cross. Feel and sense the way in which the physical, spiritual and essential realms of North impact and inform you.

Now, reach outward to the physical Above through day and night skies, to the beings of the Above in the Stellar World....and into the essential presence of the eternal Above and the power of the Transcendent. As you do this, see, sense and feel the energy within your Sacred Cross extending outward into the elemental power and presence of the Above. Commune with this elemental power through your Sacred Cross. Feel and sense the way in which the physical, spiritual and essential realms of the Above impact and inform you.

Now, reach outward to the physical Below through the bones of the Earth, to the beings of the Below in the underworld...and into the essential presence of the eternal Below and the power of the ancient, primal Earth. As you do this, see, sense and feel the energy within your Sacred Cross extending outward into the elemental power and presence of the Below. Commune with this elemental power through your Sacred Cross. Feel and sense the way in which the physical, spiritual and essential realms of the Below impact and inform you.

You are now dwelling within the form and force of your personal Sacred Cross AND the collective forms and forces of the Directions/Elements. Remain in silence...sensing the way in which your personal Sacred Cross impacts and is impacted by its relationship to the society of Directions/Elements.

To release, slowly and progressively release your co-creative relationship with the East, South, West, North...Above and Below. Sense again your own Sacred Cross. Beginning with the fourth arm, "What I Know," release and recoil this arm of your Sacred Cross back into the quiet repose of the heart. Release the third arm," Who I Am," and recoil this arm back into the quiet repose of the heart. Now release the upward extension of the second arm of the Heavens allowing it to come to rest within the heart. And finally, release the downward extension of the first arm of the Earth, letting it too come to rest within the repose of the heart. Take a few breaths to reorient your awareness to the outer world of form. Come fully into your waking awareness.

Daily Forms for Sacred Cross Work

Now that you've come to understand the three basic forms for invoking The Sacred Cross, I would like to shift our focus from the forms to the context within which the forms are used. As you know, the title of this book is "The Sacred Cross: A Transformational Spiritual Tool for Life." It was chosen because it speaks to the broad applicability of The Cross as a tool *for our lives*.

In this section we will explore how The Cross supports us in four primary contexts: 1) when we are engaged in our spiritual and magical practices, 2) when we are working with others, 3) when we face dangerous or stressful situations and 4) before we sleep at night. Though the discussions that follow speak to these four uses specifically, it is my hope that you will be inspired to discover other ways in which The Sacred Cross can serve as a transformational spiritual tool for *your* life.

The Sacred Cross in our Spiritual and Magical Work

When we are engaged in spiritual and magical activities, The Sacred Cross helps us keep the energy in our working containments and our bodies flowing cleanly. For through its use we are continually fed by the inflowing of the four-fold grace that combines the regenerative powers of the Earth, the inspiration of the Heavens, our inherent self that is "Who We Are" and our learned capabilities that are "What We Know." In addition we, and our working environments, are continuously purified by The Cross's ability to lift out any energetic build up that accumulates during our spiritual and magical work. The pristine balance of inflowing and outflowing energies achieved via our use of The Sacred Cross is no small feat. I have known many men and women of spirit who've suffered when their own resources were utilized, and then subsequently depleted, during a spiritual or magical working. Likewise, I have known practitioners who slowly and steadily lost energy and focus because their field of working accumulated too much psychic and energetic debris during a healing session, ceremony or ritual. For the most part, these situations occur because the practitioner does not understand how the subtle energies with which they are engaging can and do affect their physical body system or their field of working. Because it is so important for all men and women of spirit, let's spend a few moments discussing how devitalization occurs in our spiritual and magical work.

When we perform our spiritual and magical work ignorant of the differences between the seen worlds and the unseen worlds, we often encounter difficulty. As one of my beloved teachers used to say, the unseen world does not have to remember to eat, drink and go to the bathroom; however, we do. The primarily energy-based beings of the unseen worlds are fundamentally different from us primarily matter-based beings. When humans commune with the beings and energies of the unseen worlds, we must remember these key differences, for our interactions with the beings and energies of the unseen worlds can and do foster powerful ripples through our physical body system.

One way to care for ourselves during our otherworldly workings is to take care to perform them in a manner that is supportive of our physical, human nature. However, in caring for ourselves we must also be cautious not to inadvertently dull or stunt our capacity to sense the subtle energy currents of the unseen worlds; that would be counterproductive to the work. To put it simply, we must endeavor to work in a manner that is respectful of our humanity while not cutting ourselves off from the non-human forms and forces with which we seek to commune in the first place. Without an appropriate orientation to our humanity and the unseen worlds, we can become prone to post-spiritual/magical states of exhaustion, disorientation, self-neglect and even illness.

When we incorporate The Sacred Cross into our spiritual and magical work, we hold our humanity via the affinity of the horizontal arms to "Who We Are" and "What We Know." Likewise, we are able to meet the aims of our spiritual and magical work via the affinity of the vertical arms to the otherworldly realms of Heaven and Earth. What's more, both our humanity and otherworldly connections are held in a dynamic equilibrium within the human heart. And we know, based upon the Polarity Therapy information previously shared, that the heart possesses the power to regulate the polarity action of the primary energy field of the body. Specifically, the four-fold grace emanating from within the heart of the person invoking The Sacred Cross harmonizes the extremes of the physically-oriented seen world and energetically-oriented unseen worlds. The Earthly arm provides us access to the grounded and primal in-planet realms, while the Heavenly arm extends our consciousness toward the inspired and exalted off-planet realms. The "Who I Am" arm keeps us mindful of our essential self and so we don't ignore our bodily or personal needs. Finally, the "What I Know" arm reminds us of the tools and skills that we've picked up along the way, including the ability to exercise common sense.

When performing our spiritual and magical work, the power and presence of The Sacred Cross's four-fold grace cannot be overestimated; it is within its embrace that we are capable of receiving assistance and insight *from without us* while at the same time being well rooted *within us*. Beyond the personal benefit of the four-fold grace, there is another consideration worth mentioning in the context of our spiritual and magical work. This consideration pertains to the way in which The Sacred Cross characterizes our presence to the beings and energies that dwell within the unseen worlds.

When we are engaged in our spiritual and magical work, all we think and feel becomes part of the signature or imprint that we cast forth into the otherworlds. This signature or imprint functions like a beacon, in that it casts forth a particular quality of light and energy that informs the otherworlds as to our nature and character. From here, the law of similarities tells us that all such attributes attract their familiars and dispel their opposites. Thus as we cast forth our own energy and light, we will in turn draw to us that which is similar to our nature and repel from us that which is not. In my book, *Unseen Worlds and Practical Aspects of Spiritual Discernment,* I speak in depth about the attracting and repelling relationships among the beings and energies of the seen and unseen worlds. As this subject relates directly to all spiritual and magical work we perform, it bears mentioning in the context of The Sacred Cross. If you are interested in additional insights, the afore-mentioned book will be helpful.

Even though all human beings live on the Earth and have soul roots in the Heavens, no two people's Sacred Crosses will possess the same exact qualities. Because the way in which I connect to the deep Earth and high Heavens is somewhat unique to my own mannerisms, characteristics and life path, it will undoubtedly differ from the way in which you do the same. More so, due to their very personal nature, the horizontal arms of The Sacred Cross vary widely from person to person as well. For these reasons, each individual's Sacred Cross is unique to who they are. Remembering that our spiritual and magical work casts certain energetic qualities of character, our invocation of The Cross becomes our personal "calling card" within the unseen worlds. As each person's Cross is unique to who they are, so too is the response received from the unseen worlds. In this regard, our Sacred Cross colors the manner in which the beings and energies of the unseen worlds are attracted to or dispelled from us. This is a valuable insight for the practitioner for he or she can take from it two positive lessons. First, our Sacred Cross will assist us to attract the Inner Contacts, guides and allies that are most apt and fitting to work with us. Second, it will also assist to deflect from us that which we choose not to attract. The dynamics of attraction and repulsion lend themselves to a contemplation of personal purification, which is our next contemplation with regard to the use of The Sacred Cross in our spiritual and magical work.

Mindful of the hazards and pitfalls of "feel good spirituality," it is important to note that any spiritual or magical tool worth its salt will demand some form of personal surrender or sacrifice from the user. The Sacred Cross is no different. At first, this tool may seem like the ultimate warm and fuzzy experience. In its invocation, we feel the grounding and uplifting of Earth and Heaven as we remember our uniqueness and our learned self, which does impart a wondrous inner and outer quality of being. This is especially true when The Cross is used in times of stress or crisis. However, in keeping with its propensity to harmonize and integrate our whole body consciousness, The Sacred Cross performs another important function. When used regularly, The Cross operates in a purgative manner, in that it amplifies any personal elements or aspects that are not in harmony with the way in which the four-fold grace manifests naturally within us. For instance, if we harbor deep seated and unexpressed anger, this can create an imbalance within us. Our use of The Sacred Cross will cause this old anger to be brought to the surface where it can be acknowledged, honored and released. This clears the inner creative space so that it can instead be occupied by the expression of our Divine human nature.

As you work with The Sacred Cross, its natural purgative or purifying capacity will bring to the surface any imbalances of mind or body that are apt for purification and release. The four-fold grace of Earth, Heaven, "Who I Am" and "What I Know" is a very powerful and pure form of spiritual attunement.

Again, as like attracts like and dispels dislike, the pure attunements we bathe ourselves in challenge anything that remains out of tune within us. Though our human self can sometimes choose to continuously harbor our imbalances versus going through the discomfort of self-examination and release, our Higher Self always guides us in favor of the purification and release of our imbalances. We know that The Sacred Cross bridges the gap between reaction and right action, thus its orientation leans toward the directives of the Higher Self. Having worked with this tool for some time now, I can attest to the personal cleansing effect The Sacred Cross has on our whole body consciousness. This purification is very helpful in that it liberates our creativity and strengthens our overall health.

Persons new to this tool should understand the purgative nature of The Sacred Cross. If you find yourself presented with an opportunity to release some out-of-tune element(s) within you, and you decide to trust and surrender to the process that this tool is capable of catalyzing, you will begin to garner the transformational benefits of The Sacred Cross in real and enduring ways.

Lastly, it is also important to remember that by its very nature The Sacred Cross deemphasizes living in and through the mind in favor of living in and through the heart. Speaking from experience as a well-ensconced Capricorn thinker, this can also be a challenging transition. However, if you stay with your practices and continue your use of The Sacred Cross, this shift in consciousness will ease its way inside you as well. In all honesty, I will admit that my own work with The Sacred Cross has, at times, been demanding; and with the same candor, I will also say this work has led me to a quality of personal liberation and freedom that I am not sure I would have attained otherwise. I will also freely state that the enduring gifts I've received were worth the efforts and changes made one hundred times over.

The Sacred Cross in our Work and Life

Many of our students say they receive great personal benefit by using The Sacred Cross during their daily or working life. As you know, The Sacred Cross is a transformational spiritual tool for life; hence *life application* is part of its purpose. Frankly, if our spiritual and magical tools are not helpful in our normal daily life, they are, in my opinion, simply not helpful. In the following quotation from her practical book *The Training and Work of An Initiate*, Dion Fortune speaks to this necessity as well.

> "There tended to be a tacit assumption that (working in the world of form) was somehow inferior to that of a fully committed and fully enclosed initiate, devoted exclusively to esoteric work with no outer world distractions of family, work and friends. The view today, on the contrary, tends to see the enclosed initiate as somewhat in danger of being out of touch with the times, even to the extent of seeking a subjective refuge from the challenges of the outer world. The modern initiate is expected to take a full part in the ways of the world, striving to exemplify the spiritual life within it.[24]" – D. Fortune

For those of us whose lifestyle demands that we interact with people on a daily basis, The Sacred Cross can be a powerful tool of personal resuscitation and rebalancing. For the school

---

[24] Fortune, Dion. The Training & Work of an Initiate, Weiser Books, Boston, MA, 2000, pg. 2.

teacher or parent about to loose his or her temper with a child, The Cross grants the balance needed to move from an angry reaction to a calm and thoughtful right action. For the healer, friend or family member caretaking the physical or emotional needs of another, a periodic invocation of The Cross helps lengthen our physical, emotional and spiritual abilities, so we are better able to give of ourselves without exhaustion. For the partner who has just stepped irrevocably upon our last nerve, The Sacred Cross can grant us the ability to remain in our loving heart versus quickly careening into an intellectual couple's dispute. In all these ways and more, engaging The Sacred Cross during the day in support of all we are asked to do is immensely beneficial.

No matter what the context, when we interact with others we can unwittingly drain our own inner resources. We do this by overextending our vital body and our empathic self. Though we believe we are aiding another through these efforts, and thus we *should* do it, we often find ourselves suffering from exhaustion at the end of our efforts.

As an alternative, when we offer ourselves to another with The Cross engaged, we tap into the vast resources of Heaven and Earth, while at the same time remembering our humanity. In this way, we are not utilizing our own, limited vital energy resources; we are instead bolstered by the spiritual power of Heaven and Earth in the process. This bolstering greatly decreases the stress upon our entire physical body system.

To fully understand the benefits of working with The Sacred Cross in your daily life, I would like to suggest that you consider taking a daytime use test. It is really quite straightforward. Simply spend the next week of your life engaged as you would normally be; however, take the time to invoke The Sacred Cross once per day using The Long Form. If you are faced with a sudden stress or crisis, invoke The Sacred Cross using The Short Form. At the end of the week review all the occurred. Notice the state of your thinking, feeling and actions. Notice also your state of mind and quality of sleep. I know from my own experience that regular invocations of The Sacred Cross improve the quality of my whole body consciousness. When I forget to bolster myself with the four-fold grace of The Cross, I am not nearly as clear, creative or rested.

In all previous contexts, we've discussed our use of The Sacred Cross in a purely personal manner. However, in the course of our daily use of The Sacred Cross, we may be asked to offer its four-fold grace to another. With that possibility in mind, I would like to shift our focus from our personal use of The Sacred Cross to our gifting it in service to someone or something else. As men and women of spirit, when we work for another we endeavor to offer ourselves in service to their highest good and wholeness. The Sacred Cross is uniquely apt and fitting for this work because it both preserves the well-being of the giver and offers tangible spiritual benefit to the receiver. The manner in which The Cross is used in service to another is slightly different to the manner in which it is used for the self. Let's take a moment to explore this method and how it can be incorporated into our daily use of The Sacred Cross.

When we use The Sacred Cross for the benefit of another we do so by using a technique called "mediating spiritual power." This is a tried and true technique, often taught within the

Western Mystery Tradition. Though related to the well known relational use of the term, in a spiritual and magical context mediation has a special meaning. Mediation is a magical art form. This art form enables a person(s) to function as a physical portal or "middleperson" between two other points. Most often, one of the two other points is a human being, physical space or object in need of assistance, while the other point is the spiritual being or energy that can provide that assistance. The following quotation from W.G. Gray's "Western Inner Workings" offers us more detail.

> "A mediator of any kind is essentially a "middleman" or a "combiner of consciousness"... a human mediator is really someone who enables interaction to take place between two different classes of consciousness. Here, however, we are thinking especially of mediating purely spiritual energies along particular Paths of action."

> "The gift, power, ability, or faculty of passing on to other souls something of the spiritual energies and experience gained by contacts with higher than human consciousness – that is the type of mediatorship sought for in the Western Mysteries.[25]"

> - W.G. Gray

As men and women of spirit we can orient our consciousness toward a being or energy of the unseen worlds on behalf of another person, place or thing. Once we have oriented ourselves to the otherworldly aspect of choice, we can mediate (allow to pour through us) the essential spiritual power of that aspect into the physical world of form. As you may imagine, such mediation can be a vastly beneficial service for a brother, sister or living creature in need.

---

[25] Gray, W.G. Western Inner Workings, Sangreal Sodality Series Volume I, Samuel Weiser, Inc., York Beach, Maine, 1983.

To be clear, as humans we mediate the spiritual power of our unique essence all the time. We are always exuding the natural expressions of our individual intellect, emotions, sexuality, physicality and the like. All of our personal modes of expression transmit power and energy. So, in truth, mediation as an act is something we do, though maybe unconsciously, all the time. However, when we purposefully align ourselves to that which is higher/deeper than our purely human self we transform the common *act* of human mediation into the uncommon *art* of spiritual mediation.

Though we may be engaged in many powerful forms of spiritual work in service to others, I have come to regard the mediation of spiritual power as perhaps the purest form of sacred service we are capable of offering. I say this because most often the mediation of spiritual power happens quietly and without fanfare. As such, it does not raise the personal recognition of the man or woman of spirit as often occurs in rituals, healing sessions or workshops. In fact, in some cases the receptor and the mediator do not interact at all. We mediate spiritual power quietly, released from our desire for personal acknowledgment or accolade given to us by those we've served. Though it is a quieter, less personally aggrandizing form of sacred service, mediating spiritual power is as personally fulfilling as it is demanding. This fulfillment comes in the form of benevolent service for the sake of another human, living creature or place. The states of mind and heart that flow through benevolent service are, in my estimation, some of the highest orientations we humans are capable of attaining.

Due to its simplicity and spaciousness, The Sacred Cross is a very effective tool to use as the basis for mediating spiritual power. To employ it in this manner, we need only refocus the intent and quality of the four-fold grace it generates within and around us. Let's speak to this specifically.

As was mentioned previously, to mediate spiritual power we become a bridge or conduit between two other points: the source of spiritual power and the recipient of that power. This creates a three way junction within a direct circuit of force. This three-way junction specifies and directs the particular frequency of energy that flows forth from the four-fold grace of our Sacred Cross. I will explain how this works. Take a moment to recall a stained glass window you've seen in a church, museum or private home on a sunny day. As you know, the sunlight that exists outside is a golden yellow-white. However, on the inside, the color of that light changes as it passes through the panes of the stained glass window. Each colored pane alters the shade and vibration of the golden yellow-white sunlight passing through its kaleidoscopic array. Outside we see the unfiltered light of the sun; inside we see glorious reds, greens, blues and pinks. The light itself is the same; however, its shade and intensity changes. This same process occurs within our Sacred Cross when it is used to mediate spiritual power for the benefit of another. The focus of our consciousness toward a particular spiritual quality tempers and calibrates the shade and intensity of the four-fold grace of our Sacred Cross. This subtle adjustment of the energy generated within and emanated from our heart is felt both by us and the recipient of our mediation. Because it is a unique way of using this tool, let's walk through the mediation of spiritual power with The Sacred Cross step by step.

To use The Sacred Cross as a tool for the mediation of spiritual power, we begin by asking, or gaining permission to intuit, the needs of our recipient. If we are working on behalf of a living creature or place, we must first develop a relationship to the spirit of this being or place and then listen selflessly to discern its request of us. Next we simply invoke The Cross as we would for ourselves. In doing so either the Long or Short Form may be used. Once invoked, we direct our will, attention and sacred imagination toward making a connection to the spiritual presence requested. If, for instance, our recipient asks for the quality of "peace" to be given to them, we employ our will, attention and sacred imagination to create a clear attunement to the forms and forces of peace that exist within the creative worlds around us. The efforts of our attunement can be directed toward the intra-planetary, surface and/or off-planet reservoirs of peace. From here, we invite the peace we've attuned to into our heart where the arms of the Cross are already co-mingling. As we do this, the four-fold grace of our Sacred Cross becomes impregnated by our attunement to peace. Finally, we again employ our will, attention and sacred imagination to project the four-fold grace of our Cross, saturated with peace, toward the etheric body of the recipient. As we do, we see, sense and feel the spiritual power of peace leaving our heart and in rapping itself gently around the etheric body of the recipient in a soft cloud or blanket-like form.

I want to clarify that in our projection of the spiritual power to which we've attuned, we should focus upon the etheric body of the recipient. When working with a living creature or human being, it is best not to project the essence of the helpful presence at their physical body. Instead we offer it to the etheric body that exists a few inches beyond their physical form. In this way, the chosen spiritual power enters their personal sphere without encroaching upon the physical body as that can be inappropriately direct. Once within the personal sphere of the recipient, their own etheric body will determine how best to incorporate the quality into the whole physical body system.

Let us consider a particular example. Say, for instance, you are working with an upset child and they tell you that feeling safe would be most helpful for them now. After your invocation of The Cross, you would connect to the spiritual essence of safety beyond you both. Next, you would allow your heart center to be filled with the qualities of "safety" and all the spiritual powers that align with and work through that word. From here, focus on the space beyond the physical body of the child. Now simply mediate or radiate the spiritual power of "safety" to this young being.

This manner of focused mediation is one of the most powerful uses of The Sacred Cross. Often in our classes we will pair two individuals together, letting one talk about their life to the listener in the normal conversational manner. Then, we ask the talker to continue his or her conversation while the listener invokes The Cross on their behalf. During the pre-Cross round of sharing it feels like a normal conversation. However, when The Cross is invoked and a spiritual presence is mediated by the listener to the speaker, the people, the conversation and even the room changes.

In situations involving non-human beings, our task is different but similar. If you are a gardener The Sacred Cross is a wonderful tool to incorporate into your soil tilling, planting and harvesting. Take tilling the soil, for instance. In this situation we wish to fortify the health of our land and eventual harvest. To begin, we determine what qualities we wish to till into the soil as we prepare it to receive the seed. Good qualities to attune to in this instance include fertility, creativity and receptivity. Likewise, one may attune to their farming ancestors or an aspect of the Goddess apt for soil working, such as Sheela na Gig, Fortuna or Brigit. Once chosen, The Sacred Cross is invoked and the quality or spirit contact is attuned to via our will, attention and sacred imagination, creating a circuit of force between the spiritual power, our Cross and the soil. From here, simply open your heart and till the soil with the spiritual power of your chosen attunement streaming through your heart into the soil beneath your feet. Any faery allies who populate your garden will undoubtedly appreciate this and respond.

For animal lovers, The Sacred Cross can help us to tend to the needs of our beloved companion(s). If, for instance, we are trying to help a pet who must visit the veterinarian, knowing what anxiety this causes in our animal friends, using The Sacred Cross to mediate the spiritual power of peace, calming and trust can be very helpful both for them and for us.

Though less verbal in their ability to give direct feedback, the mediation of spiritual power we offer to an animal, plant, body of water or mountain top is just as powerful as that offered to a human being. As you begin to offer your sacred service in this way, you will come to feel their subtle appreciation as well.

In any situation where our resources feel drained, pressured or stressed, The Sacred Cross is nothing short of a small miracle. I would like to mention a use that, though thankfully not daily in origin, is something of a true Sacred Cross miracle. During the

2006 Lebanon/Israel War, several of our Women of Vision participant's homes were threatened by bombs and gunfire. In response, they had to leave their homes and gather in their community bomb shelters. Our anxiety was great as we waited to hear if our beloved friends were safe. Eventually and with great gratitude, we received the news that they were indeed safe. In this same communication we also received a surprising gift. Time in the shelters was frightening; and at one particular point the people gathered were quite distraught. One of our Women of Vision ladies realized that she could offer something to the group to help calm their anxiety: The Sacred Cross. The four-fold grace of The Sacred Cross offered safety and security in the face of a life-threatening event. Though it is my hope that someday we will no longer need to test our spiritual tools within the context of war, I was very moved by the use of The Cross in this manner.

Whether we are engaged in the routine of our life or navigating a special circumstance, our spiritual and magical tools should be simple and profound enough to support us. We are souls embodied upon this Earth for a reason, and that reason is to fully experience the world of form without forgetting our Divine origins. The Sacred Cross provides a stable foundation for both aspects of the human experience in its ability to bless us with the four-fold grace while also keeping us fully present in the face of the challenges and opportunities of any given moment. This, I feel, is the most profound gift, uniquely given through this particular spiritual tool. In this sense, we have one additional application to explore, the use of The Sacred Cross in our sleep. As sleep practices are performed less frequently by men and women of spirit these days, I would like to address this application in depth.

The Sacred Cross in Sleep

Somewhere in the distant past humans lived in constant union with the greater consciousnesses they inhabited. This union created between themselves and the whispers of the trees, breath of the creatures and remembrance of the stars permeated their lives, day and night. Through the daily practices of their waking life many men and women of spirit are endeavoring to remember their constant union with the greater consciousness within which they live. However, surprisingly, few of them pay attention to the companion rhythms of the night. Deep within the recesses of our human experience there is a collective memory where our union with the night forces and the pre-sleep rites is stored. Without access to these recesses lying dormant within us, many men and women of spirit simply fall into bed night after night hoping that the quality of sleep that ensues will be enough to resuscitate them for the coming day. Because this is true for so many of us, let's thoroughly consider the virtues of courting sacred sleep.

Medical professionals often say that, on average, humans need between seven to eight hours of rest per night to allow the body to complete its daily restoration and rejuvenation processes. When we stop to consider how those seven to eight hours compare to the twenty-four hours available within a day, we quickly realize that we spend almost one-third of our lives in sleep. As I began my spiritual and magical training, this statistic fostered the following questions within me:

o   Is our body's need for rest and recovery the only reason we require sleep?

o   If we come into a body to experience the world of form why is it that we spend one-third of our lives disconnected from the world of form via sleep?

o   Is there a deeper mystery to sleep that we should be considering as men and women of spirit?

The answers to these questions are found within ties that bind our sleep cycle to our remembrance of the greater intelligence within the night force, and the way our connection to that intelligence informs our soul's growth. To appreciate these ties, we must understand the magical capacity of the sleep cycle.

When we sleep significant aspects of our consciousness leave the physical world of form, making their nightly journey into the sublunar, solar and sometimes even stellar realms of consciousness. Through this journey our consciousness comes into contact with the beings and energies that occupy these realms. Though they are always available to us, our nighttime connection with the lunar, solar and stellar realms of consciousness is quite strong because, for the most part, during the daytime hours our minds and bodies are focused toward our waking life. If we improve our relationship between the night forces, the three realms and our human consciousness, we will experience the gifts that come to us through deeper sleep and dream states. It is within these deeper states that we realize that there is more to our night work than the complete restoration of the physical body. We find that, in addition, we can also experience a complete restoration, and remembrance, of our divinely human or soul consciousness. To ensure commonality in our understanding of the three places visited during our nightly journeys, let's take a moment to explore the dynamics of the sublunar, solar and stellar realms.

Located just beyond the physical Earth, we find the zone of physical space and spiritual consciousness known as the sublunar realm. Due to its proximity to the Earth, this realm is relatively "dense" and as such contains a great variety of spiritual and psychic activity; some of this activity is helpful and some not. As it harbors a great deal of activity in a relatively concentrated space, our relationship to the sublunar realm varies. At times we dance within an intuitive connection to the grace of an incoming soul destined for a powerful and love-filled life. At other times we come into contact with the dissonance of the regret, disorientation and fear of exiting souls. In addition to introducing us to the vast array of spiritual and psychic activity within it, the sublunar realm dreamscapes also possess an affinity for and thus illuminate the psychological terrain within us, guiding us toward a better understanding of ourselves. In general, it is helpful to remember that the dreamscapes of the sublunar realm immerse us within the spiritual territory that lies closest to the physical world of form, both personally and collectively.

If and when our nightly journey takes us beyond the sublunar realm, we encounter what is known as the solar and stellar realms. The solar and stellar dreamscapes put us in direct contact with the exalted spiritual beings and energies that exist off planet. These contacts possess the power and insight to shape and change our whole body consciousness in positive and helpful ways.

Many spiritual traditions teach us that, if navigated mindfully, the landscapes we traverse in sleep prepare us for the landscapes we will traverse upon our death. Our nightly rhythm of leaving and returning to the physical world of form creates an imprint within us that prepares us for the time when we will leave and not return (to this particular body.) If we have a relationship to the spiritual forces of the solar and stellar realms while we live, our post-life journey through the sublunar realm will be much easier.

When seen and understood in light of these realms and their potential to affect our consciousness, the importance of sleep becomes elevated. In this light we realize that sleep should be given the same reverence that we more readily offer to our daytime practices. To do this, we must learn to cultivate a healthy relationship among these three personal aspects: our physical body system, the night forces and the realms we journey to and through. Fortunately, this cultivation can be achieved by using The Sacred Cross as our sleep practice. To discover how this tool enhances our sleeping life, let's begin by exploring the relationship between the night forces and The Cross.

As you may have already perceived, our invocation of The Sacred Cross does not *manifest* the Earth, Heavens, "Who We Are" and "What We Know;" they are always there within and beyond our human form. Instead, our invocation of The Sacred Cross affirms and reconnects us to what's already there, all around and within us, all the time. If The Sacred Cross affirms and reconnects us to *what's already there*, it stands to reason that as what's there shifts and changes, our Sacred Cross shifts and changes in response. We know from experience, that *what's there* during the daytime is quite different from *what's there* at night.

During the day the dominant presence of the Sun brings heat, light and vigor to the environment, awakening the solar qualities within and all around us. During the night, the dominant presence of the darkened sky brings coolness, quiet and repose, awakening the lunar qualities within and all around us. You need only pray, meditate, engage in ritual or invoke your Cross during the day and again at night to gain a visceral understanding of just how different it feels to work within these opposite forces.

Our body's ability to let go of its attachment to the day force, and instead attach itself to the night force, is the key to good quality sleep. In the day force our minds are occupied with the lists, people, tasks, responsibilities and projects that constitute the rhythms of the daytime. In contrast, in the night force our waking mind relaxes and surrenders to the quieted, journeying mind. The inability to make the transition between the day force and the night force keeps many of us tied to substances and supplements that coerce our bodies into sleep. If used repeatedly, these sleep aids can actually circumvent our natural sleep cycle, making our bodies dependent upon them for rest. Any substance that alters the body's relationship to the natural sleep cycle alters the nighttime journey. If we repeatedly rely on substances for sleep, our innate connection to and acceptance of the currents of the night force and the sublunar, solar and stellar realms is circumvented. Through The Sacred Cross sleep practice we learn how to embrace the night force and cultivate the natural sleep rhythms within us, thus substantively improving the quality of our rest and the quality of our nighttime journey through the realms beyond the physical world of form.

Just as the rhythmic repetition of our sacred daily practices builds strong spiritual muscles within us, the rhythmic repetition of our sacred nighttime practices builds the same. Over the years I have experimented with using and not using my sleep practice. What I have noticed is when I perform my simple ten minute nighttime sleep practice, I rest deeply, experience helpful dreams and rise easier the next morning.

To improve your relationship with the night forces and increase your working relationship with the sublunar, solar and stellar realms, I invite you to create a sleep practice for yourself. The following italicized text describes a simple Sacred Cross sleep practice. The recorded version of this meditation is the last track on CD II. As you develop your own sleep practice, simply play this track while you lie in bed at night. As it is the final track, your player should stop at its conclusion, thus preserving the soft embrace of the Sacred Cross sleep practice with ease.

The Sacred Cross Sleep Practice

Lying down in bed, upon your back[26], prepared for sleep, sense the way in which the back of your body rests parallel to the Earth below you and the front of your body rests parallel to the Heavens above you. Allow your body consciousness to take in the new way in which your body interacts with the forces of Heaven and Earth at night.

Sense the night forces that exist all around you. Sense the quieted pulse of the resting Earth... and the soft radiance of the

---

[26] For the most part, The Sacred Cross sleep practice works best when we lie on our back. However, I have known students who feel discomfort on their back and thus do this meditation lying on their side. While I feel that lying on the back is best, as it puts the body in a more natural state of "behind and before," please discover and do what works best for you.

starlit night sky. In this awareness simply breathe, drawing in the breath that brings the peace and quiet of the night force within you. And exhale, releasing the preoccupations of the day...for the day is now done.

On an expansive exhale, send the taproot within your heart into the deep, quieted Earth. On a contracting inhale, pull the still and steady presence of the deep Earth toward you, allowing it to pool all along the underside of your body from head to heel. Surrender to the night forces and your constant connection to the deep Earth.

On an expansive exhale, send the taproot within your heart upward into the glistening night sky that hovers above you. Climb until you reach the realm of the high Heavens. On a contracting inhale, pull the calming reassurance of the Heavens toward you, allowing it to pool all along the surface of your body from head to toe. Surrender to the night forces and your constant connection to the high Heavens.

On the contraction of an inhale, go deep within you, rousing the "Who I Am" arm of your Sacred Cross. On an expansive exhale, allow this arm to gently open outward along the plane of the quiet Earth and beneath the night sky. Breathing in and out ... let the relaxed and open arm of "Who I Am" surrender to the night forces in rest and receptivity.

On the contraction of an inhale, go deep within you, rousing the "What I Know" arm of your Sacred Cross. On an expansive exhale, allow this arm to gently open outward along the plane of the quiet Earth and beneath the night sky. Breathing in and out ... let the relaxed and open arm of "What I Know" surrender to the night forces in rest and receptivity.

As you will soon discover, the Sacred Cross sleep practice fosters a very different kind of rest. In its embrace, the deeper tones of the Earth and softer tones of the Heavens co-mingle with the knowing and being of the self. In addition, there is a greater ease to the way in which wisdom and insight is offered within the context of our dreams and visitations. When I perform the Sacred Cross sleep practice, it is as if I am enfolded within the soft and powerful embrace of a greater intelligence. When I need information about my coming day or my Priestess work, the nighttime Sacred Cross gently connects me to the forms and forces of the otherworlds where this information is available. When no such information is needed, I simply sleep in the embrace of the deep Earth and high Heavens in a restful remembrance of "Who I Am" and "What I Know". What I find remarkable is that even when information needs to be conveyed, the dreams and visitations that come do not compromise my rest in any way. This was quite a welcome change.

The Sacred Cross you invoke at the beginning of your sleep cycle does not have to be formally released upon waking. The beauty of a sleep practice is that it rides the currents of your body's natural rhythms in right relationship to the night and day rhythms. As the dawn approaches, The Cross slowly and steadily dissolves. Because it is a night practice, the presence of the coming Sun opens out the energy. The same is also true of our day time practices, as darkness comes their prominence within our consciousness fades as well. This is why it is best to have both waking and sleeping practices; as they work differently upon our daytime and nighttime consciousness.

If the concept of a sleep practice is new for you, consider this simple consciousness training technique. Prepare your bedroom by burning a peaceful, night force incense prior to climbing into bed. Once in bed, perform your Sacred Cross sleep practice. Then, upon waking, rise out of bed and burn an enlivening, day force incense. For this technique to work, it is important to make your night and day incense choices and stick to them. You are training your body consciousness via your sense of smell, so the medium must be consistent with no substitutions. Personally, I burn sweetgrass prior to sleep to bring on the blessings of the night force and white sage in the morning to enliven the day force within me.

With the sleep practice method of invocation in place, the fundamentals of daily applications of The Sacred Cross are complete. As mentioned in the introduction to this book, we will now explore the esoteric foundations of The Sacred Cross.

Part 3: Questions and Reflections

The questions and reflections for Part 3 are based on the personal observations made during your initial invocations of The Sacred Cross. As such, they will serve as a benchmark against which you may gauge your future progress with the forms introduced in this section. To receive the most benefit from these exercises, it is important to be detailed and thorough in your answers. Think of the words you write as notes in a bottle to yourself.

1. Write a detailed description of your first few experiences using The Long Form for invoking The Sacred Cross. Be sure to include both positive and challenging experiences, certainties and points of confusion.

2. Write a detailed description of your first few experiences using The Short Form for invoking The Sacred Cross. Be sure to include both positive and challenging experiences, certainties and points of confusion.

3. Make a few notes as to your personal use of The Sacred Cross during your normal, waking life. This may include instances of use in your work, with your family and friends or for yourself. Be sure to record your physical and emotional state before, during and after the working.

4. Write a detailed description of your first few experiences invoking The Sacred Cross before sleep. Note both your quality of sleep and any dreams that came during the night. Be sure to include both positive and challenging experiences, certainties and points of confusion with this working as well.

Part 4: Esoteric Aspects of The Sacred Cross

To begin, let's define our use of the word esoteric, as it is a term that means different things to different people.

> **"Esoteric** *adj.* designed for or understood by the specially initiated alone, of or relating to knowledge that is restricted to a small group."

> **"Esoteric** *adj.* (of a philosophical doctrine or the like) intended to be revealed only to the initiates of a group: *the esoteric doctrines of Pythagoras* and the *"tae so* and *tae exo in Plato's The First Alcibiades*[27]"

According to these dictionary references, the word esoteric refers to knowledge that is restricted to a select few. In the practical definition found in the literature that incorporates it, the word esoteric is also used to describe the spiritual or religious practices of those whose loosely-related roots stretch back to the doctrines of Pythagoras and Plato.

In *The First Alcibiades,* Plato uses the terms "ta esó" meaning the inner things and "ta exó" meaning the outside things. Further, "eso" is the root and basis of the word esoteric. In my research I found that, in general, it is believed that that "ta esó" refers to the pursuit of wisdom that requires a certain measure of inwardness, while "ta exó" refers to the wisdom that is readily apparent upon an external examination. As this incidence in Plato's writing is often used as the probable first appearance of "eso" and knowing that modern dictionaries often misrepresent words of art, it is important to explore the literary and spiritual use of this term. One need only go so far as to look up the words "pagan" and "witch" to see just how

---

[27] Webster's Seventh Collegiate Dictionary, Wikipedia, Dictionary.com.

misrepresented words of art are in what is supposed to be a non-biased reference text.

As used within the true and abiding spiritual contexts, the term esoteric refers to a body of experience-based knowledge that a practitioner may accumulate via diligent spiritual work and apprenticeship. The key here is the phrase "experience-based knowledge." As any accomplished man or woman of spirit will tell you, true and enduring esoteric wisdom cannot be accumulated by reading books about spirituality or by examining the *surface* of things. Though our studies certainly help, true and enduring esoteric wisdom can only be accumulated through the personal acquisition of experience-based knowledge. Thus "eso" actually refers to that which lives within us, placed there through the challenges and gains of our own personal experiences.

In summary, the word esoteric is not used to denote the coveted achievements of a class of spiritually elite persons. Rather, it is used to convey the understanding that it requires a measure of personal relationship and dedication to acquire spiritual wisdom; and few persons are willing to invest at that level. This same analogy can be applied to friendship. It takes time, presence and sincere commitment to develop the kind of friendships that truly support us in our lives. Our spiritual and magical practices are no different. It is true that many aspects of esoteric wisdom are hidden from view for those who are only interested in surface relationships to the unseen worlds. Is this not also what separates acquaintances from true friends? In the context of our work with The Sacred Cross, the word esoteric refers to the experience-based wisdom, pertinent to any spiritual or magical tradition, that is accumulated through the sincere application of the practitioner.

To date, the esoteric aspects of The Sacred Cross have not yet been formally taught. In part, this is because the sincere application of its practitioners had not evolved to the point of their revealing. On the eve of the eighth year of its use, I am happy to offer my personal experience-based knowledge of The Sacred Cross to the current and new practitioners of this wonderful tool. I trust that, consistent with every other aspect of The Cross, my understanding of these esoteric applications will continue to grow. For now, I offer you what I know to be true of its esoteric nature; I welcome the eventual communication of your own insights and discoveries.

To begin our journey, we greet and pay homage to the guardian at the veil: The High Priestess (pictured). Cloaked in light blue draped fabrics cascading down toward the crescent moon that rests at her feet, The High Priestess guards the threshold separating this world from the otherworlds. Positioned between the pillar of boaz/dark/severity and the pillar of jachin/light/mercy, she *is* the coveted "middle pillar" where the balanced way between the paths of mercy and severity dwells. Looking closer at her, we see that she is crowned with the diadem and the four phases of the moon (the dark phase being behind the full moon, and thus out of view.) In her lap she holds a copy of the Torah, partly revealed and partly concealed, conveying its esoteric nature.

Just above her lap, resting quietly upon the breast and heart of The High Priestess, we see The Sacred Cross itself.

As we move beyond the veils she guards, making our way into the esoteric nature of The Sacred Cross, The High Priestess serves us; for she stands at this threshold in balance. If any of the deeper, esoteric aspects of The Sacred Cross presented beyond this point seem unclear or out of reach, simply return to this threshold and spend time meditating upon her form. As the guardian at the threshold, she possesses the power and presence to assist us in our navigation of the otherworlds and the internal changes that can be catalyzed by our use of special spiritual tools such as The Sacred Cross.

Over the course of the last three years I've engaged in a series of meditations with the intention of deepening my understanding and experience of The Sacred Cross. During these meditations new and significant aspects of this tool's capacities were revealed. Once received and recorded in my journal, I began an exploration of several instructional texts within the Western Mystery Tradition where the esoteric principles that correspond to my meditative experiences are generally discussed. In relaying both, I will begin with the visions/meditations and then progress to their esoteric foundations.

The principles of reincarnation tell us that the soul comes to the Earth several times to experience the physical world in human form. Many occult and mystical teachings contend that in between human lives, the soul journeys to and through places in consciousness that exist amid the involutionary (coming into embodiment) and evolutionary (leaving embodiment) cycles.

Based upon its need to grow and evolve, the soul's journey between lives consists of both a review of the prior life and a determination of the next life. This process can take several years. In preparation for the next incarnation, the soul and its Divine support assess the right time, place, astrological imprint and human story for its next incarnation. While the historical context, embodiment and human story changes from lifetime to lifetime, the soul's wisdom and experience is continuous and cumulative. Through my own invocations and meditations with The Sacred Cross, I came to understand that there is a special, alchemical magic that occurs within us as we sit in the center of the Earthly extension of the first arm and the Heavenly extension of the second arm. Through this magic, our human, current life consciousness is slowly and steadily imbued with our soul's cumulative knowledge. Let me explain what I mean.

The Earth extension connects us to the deep spiritual impulses of the planet. As we know, to experience this world of form it is to the Earth that we return incarnation after incarnation. The first arm of The Sacred Cross connects us to the Earth, the place that has held and witnessed each one of our many lives in the world of form. It is, in essence, the receptor and witness of our soul's growth.

The Heavenly extension of the second arm connects us to that which we revere the most: our "holy of holies". As such it unites us to the Divine spark from which we derive our soul's very essence. The Heavenly arm of The Sacred Cross reunites us with the spiritual home we rest within between each physical life and thus reconnects us to the stored imprints and memories housed within our soul.

The Heavens are where we spend our time in between lives in spirit form; the Earth is where we begin and end each life in physical form. Thus the vertical arms of The Sacred Cross work together to create a bridge of continuity that helps our consciousness transcend the perspective of this one life by reuniting us with the Heavens that inspire and the Earth that witnesses all of the lives we have lived. The word that was offered in meditation in reference to the combined ability of the vertical arms of The Sacred Cross was "eternal."

I then came to understand that special alchemical magic occurs within us when we sit within the embrace of the horizontal arms of The Sacred Cross. The horizontal arms focus our consciousness upon the essential expression of our current human form. One arm holds the unique qualities of our natal patterning, our likes and dislikes, our human personality. The other arm holds the accumulated skills, tools and knowledge that we have gained throughout this human life. The horizontal arms of "Who I Am" and "What I Know" act as the repository for this unique life. Simply put, they harbor all of the imprints made upon the soul within this one incarnation. The word that came in meditation to represent the combined capacity of the horizontal arms of The Cross was "incarnal."

As we know, both the vertical and horizontal arms unite within the meeting place of the human heart which has the ability to harmonize polarities within the physical body system. What is being revealed by this new awareness of the magic encased within each of these extensions? Through my progressive meditations, I was coming to understand that the esoteric nature of The Sacred Cross is to catalyze the sacred union of the eternal soul and the incarnated self (or, in other words, the conscious being of this lifetime and the conscious being that transcends lifetimes.) Many men and women of spirit suffer from the inner tug-of-war that occurs between their human self and their Divine self. Over the years, I have counseled several who found it very difficult to move beyond the conditions of their human story to find a higher expression of themselves to access. By the same token, I have advised others who did not, in any way, feel comfortable in the physical world and instead deeply desired to escape back into the embrace of the soul's knowing they remembered so strongly. When I realized that the esoteric nature of The Sacred Cross offered a tool to guide the soul forces and the human embodiment into harmony and balance for the individual, I became very excited indeed! This new discovery led me on an exploratory journey into the teachings of the Western Mystery Tradition where matters like these are contemplated. I began my search within the mythos of the Ancient Egyptians and their principles pf reincarnation.

In many orthodox and non-orthodox spiritual traditions, the process of coming into physical form is understood to constitute a major transition for the soul. During this transition, the soul becomes separated from the Divine consciousness and corresponding complete remembrance of the Self it formerly knew. The soul descends through the higher realms of consciousness into the lower realms of consciousness where it meets the elemental embrace of the Earth, Air, Fire and Water that come together to form our physical body. In its previous state of Divine union, the soul was one with Mother/Father God; after its descent there is a distinct sense of separation from this union. Those of us who dedicate aspects of our lives to spiritual and magical practices endeavor to remember and reunite our life-based consciousness with the soul's awareness of the Divine union. In some traditions we are instructed that our ultimate remembrance or "enlightenment" can only occur when we ascend, leaving the human body behind. In the Western Mystery Tradition this ideal is not achieved in this manner; it is instead accomplished by rediscovering the Divine union while still embodied within the world of form, bringing Heaven to Earth while lifting Earth up into Heaven.

With this as our basis, let us move on to the Egyptian myth of Isis, Osiris and Set. Osiris was a great and benevolent king of Egypt, Isis was his faithful queen and Set the evil brother and rival of Osiris. While masterminding a plan to rid himself of his kingly brother, Set secretly measured Osiris' body in an effort to fashion a coffin in his exact physical proportions. At a banquet that soon followed, Set promised to give this exquisite and much admired coffin to the one whose body it most suitably fit. Last of all the guests to try the coffin was Set's inconspicuous brother Osiris, who of course fit the casket perfectly. Once inside, Set and his co-conspirators swiftly nailed the coffin shut and then poured boiling lead upon its surface to seal all air holes, thus securing death of the one within. Once sealed, the coffin containing Osiris was set adrift upon the Nile.

Isis was soon informed of her beloved husband's fate and thus set forth to find him. Believing him to be dead, she endeavored to ensure his funeral rites were performed so that his soul could rest. After a long and exhaustive search, Isis found the coffin of Osiris lodged in a wooden pillar used to uphold the roof in a local country king's abode. She offered herself as nurse to the king's son while waiting for the right time to divulge her true purpose. When the time came, she revealed herself as the great queen she was, and beseeched the king for the pillar and coffin. Arriving home with both, she was overcome with tears of grief and sorrow. In this state, she mated with the body of her husband and conceived their child Horus. Soon Set discovered the coffin's reemergence. Enraged, he immediately seized the body of Osiris, cut it into many pieces and scattered it all about the land. In mourning, Isis wandered the land collecting together the fragments of her beloved. In the end, she found all but one, his organ of generation[28].

To most, this famous Egyptian myth characterizes the great mysteries of regeneration and rebirth. In his book *A History of White Magic*[29], Gareth Knight offers a lesser-known interpretation of the Isis/Osiris myth. In addition to being seen as a tale of regeneration and rebirth, Knight tells us Osiris can also be seen as a representative of the human race leaving unity with the Divine (i.e. kingly state of innocence) and coming into human form (i.e. being nailed into the coffin). The subsequent dismemberment and dispersion of the body of Osiris is likened to the loss of people from their primal unity to the Divine. To restore our collective loss, we await the benevolent mother Goddess who endlessly seeks to find every piece of the divided human soul, so we may all return to Divine unity once again. Knight's interpretation of the famous myth speaks to the journey each seeker must take toward the reestablishment of their union between the self (human consciousness) and Self (Divine consciousness). Separated from this union we are forgetful of not only our own Divinity but of the Divine in

---

[28] Budge, E. A. Wallis, *Egyptian Ideas of the Afterlife*, Dover Publications Inc., New York 1995. Spence, Lewis, *Myths and Legends of Egypt*, Studio Editions, London, 1990.
[29] Knight, Gareth. *A History of White Magic*, Mowbrays London and Oxford, 1978.

general. Those of us capable of deeper spiritual work apply ourselves toward the remembrance and recollection of our human self and Divine origins.

Dion Fortune referenced this same principle in a slightly different, but compatible, manner. In her books *Applied Magic* and *The Esoteric Philosophy of Love and Marriage* she discusses the importance of our individual reunification with Divine consciousness. I will offer a brief synopsis of her work.

Again relying upon the assertions of reincarnation, she reiterates the well known occult principles of the seven-fold body of man. Fortune explains that the three highest bodies constitute the Individuality; they are the spark of pure spirit, the concrete spiritual nature and the abstract mind. The four lower bodies make up the Personality; they include the concrete mental, emotional/astral, passional/etheric and the physical body. Individuality, Fortune comments, is the Unit of Evolution while the Personality is the Unit of Incarnation. She reasons that the Personality is built up to enable the Individuality to experience embodiment, which provides the nourishment that enables the soul's growth. The aim of a life is for the Personality to be experienced and then released by being uplifted and integrated into the Individuality, thus uniting our lower self/Personality with our Higher Self/Individuality.

Gareth Knight and Dion Fortune were by no means the first to write about such theories. Traveling further back along the taproot of the Western Mysteries, we find the same esoteric foundations of Individuality and Personality in the work of the Neoplatonic philosopher Plotinus (204-270 C.E.) In *The Six Enneads* which was composed and edited by his pupil, Porphyry, Plotinus asserts that the soul is composed of a

Higher Self and a Lower Self. The Higher Self moves lifetime to lifetime, while the Lower Self is the seat of a life's personality. According to Plotinus, the Higher Self is not known directly or consciously to the Lower Self during the life; instead it nourishes and guides the Lower Self from above. He believed that when embodied in the human form, the soul was in a state of alienation from itself and from its Source. This is due, in part, to the human will to self-possess which, in his estimation, takes the task too far by accidentally divorcing itself from its memory of and connection to its own Divine origins. He asserts that we cannot fully know ourselves without knowing our origins in the transcendent Divine[30]. To Plotinus, the human soul is noble; further, he believed that union with the soul while embodied was not an insurmountable feat. Rather, through reflective contemplation (e.g. the upliftment of mental occupation toward the Divine intelligence via active meditation), man could again find union with his soul[31].

We know that Plotinus' work referred to Plato's work which referred to Socrates' work; thus why credit him with this important assertion? It is true that we could find similar assertions in the work of Plato or Socrates; however, Plotinus' self and soul reflections exhibit a rare quality of first hand experience. Upon reading Plotinus, one gets the impression that this man walked his esoteric talk, for only a true mystic can offer keys to the inner landscapes in such a manner.

I'm sure by now you're making the connections between the meditative insights I shared previously and these teachings

---

[30] O'Daly, Gerard J. P., Plotinus' Philosophy of Self, Irish University Press, Shannon Ireland, 1973.
[31] O'Brien, Elmer S.J. The Essential Plotinus, Hackett Publishing Company, 1964.

within the Western Mystery Tradition. To summarize, The Sacred Cross creates a heart-centered meeting place for the Eternal/Individuality and the Incarnal/Personality. As such, through its use, we can be guided toward the reunification of our self (human incarnal consciousness) and our Self (Divine eternal consciousness). In laypersons terms, The Sacred Cross allows us to reunify the Divine Spark of our soul with our current human form. Such unification can ease a great deal of confusion and suffering felt by many men and women who feel alienated from either their soul knowing or human nature. In addition, this unification assists us in the preparation for both our death and eventual rebirth.

Though our deeper, esoteric exploration has focused upon the personal aspects and attributes of The Sacred Cross, it does not end here. For there are equally profound elements of transpersonal work embedded within the mysteries and magic of The Cross.

Transpersonal Use of The Sacred Cross

Thus far in this book, we have discussed The Cross's ability to recalibrate and resource us in many different ways via this tool's capacity to foster an expanded state of awareness within us. In our use of The Cross a meeting place is created in our heart where the four-fold grace of Earth, Heaven, "Who We Are" and "What We Know" emerges, guiding us toward a clearer sense of right action. In a second sense, I have spoken to the esoteric applications of The Cross as one meditative means through which we may eventually achieve a state of remembrance and reunification between our Eternal/Individuality and our Incarnal/Personality. These are the personal applications of The Sacred Cross. We have also worked to establish the foundation for the relational or societal aspects of The Sacred Cross by revealing its compatibility with the Directions and Elements. At this point, I would like to reveal to you the transpersonal application of The Sacred Cross. To begin, I will address a new and reoccurring phenomenon taking place within my Seership practice.

Since 1995, I have worked as a hereditary Seer or intuitive within my community. For the first eleven years of my practice, I noticed no real trends to speak of among the clients whom I advised on various issues and occasions. However, in 2006 a remarkable new pattern began to emerge among my clients. To be clear, my client base consists of about seventy percent return clients and thirty percent new clients. So throughout the course of my practice, I have seen several clients repeatedly. Normally, I begin by performing an initial unaided reading. Then I scrutinize the intuitions received using an objective cross-check system; for this I use the Rider/ Waite/Smith Tarot oracle. Since 2006, one single card has mysteriously reappeared over and over again within the context of my readings for different clients. Because this was such an unusual occurrence, I spent some time meditating upon the reason for its ubiquitous display. What I learned was quite remarkable.

Many of us are familiar with the spiritual predictions and astrological alignments associated with the year 2012. Leading up to this grand mark in history we are experiencing many significant global changes as we are, in fact, already living within the force of this alignment. The climate fluctuations facing our planet have recently been deemed nearly irreversible. Several countries' economic health is suffering as the capitalistic materialism we've practiced for the past two hundred years meets its end. All the while a heightened threat of nuclear armament looms continually within the conflicted nations of the Fertile Crescent and Far East. Most of us are quite clear that big changes are afoot; however, the breadth of our clarity begins and ends there. So much is changing at the same time, how will humanity rise to meet the magnitude and complexity that faces us now? Within this particular global context, the one Tarot card that offers its guidance to my clients again and again, with nearly alarming reliability, is *The Star*. I believe part of the answer to the aforementioned question resides within the message of this card.

If you are familiar with the Tarot, you know that *The Star* connects us to off-planet, stellar wisdom. You may also know that *The Star* was intentionally reordered within the sequence of the Rider/Waite/Smith deck. It actually belongs after the Moon and Sun, consistent with the Qabalistic teachings that form part of this oracle's foundation. In its proper placement and interpretation, *The Star* represents our access to the Divine impulse that supports our embodiment. In this, it mirrors the impetus just discussed with regard to the merging of the Individuality and Personality within the life. In sequence, *The Star* is positioned just before our liberating release in *Judgment* and reunification with the Divine in *The World*, thus completing the Fool's Earthly journey. *The Star* presents itself when it is time for the seeker to reach far beyond the routine of his or her habit-body fortified lifestyle and access that which is inscribed upon the life by the pen of the soul.

Since 2006, I have seen this card repeatedly in my readings for clients. I have come to understand that its presence signifies a swift move beyond the era of the individuated human consciousness and toward the era of the remembered human collective. The message of *The Star* is well summarized by G.H. Soro, Q.L.:

> "The Star shows the seven-pointed Venus shining about
> the waters of Aquarius (the water/future human), the
> guiding force of love in all its forms and that the binds of
> Saturn are dissolved in the purified Waters of Baptism.
> The dove of the Spirit hovers above the Tree of
> Knowledge giving the promise of ultimate attainment –
> and on the other side gleams the Tree of Life[32]"

In other words, the old forms of structure are dissolving in the purified waters of a lovingly and divinely inspired greater evolution; all that once made sense within the context of an inspired and prudent life no longer applies. A new imprint is required. We must cultivate and operate from the meeting place between our personal Incarnal/Eternal work and the collective Incarnal/Eternal work of humanity. Those of us willing to reach for *The Star* do so now in a gesture of ambassadorship; we are representatives of humanity, not only as individuals working to achieve a reunification with our Eternal/ Individuality and our Incarnal/ Personality, but also with the same aspects of the human race as a collective.

How does this relate to The Sacred Cross specifically? When you create the form and force of The Sacred Cross, you unite your body consciousness with the Earth, Heavens, "Who You Are" and "What You Know" within your individual heart. What *The Star* teaches us is this is no longer enough; we must

---

[32] Regardie, Israel. The Golden Dawn: 6th Edition, Lewellyn Worldwide Publications, 2003, p 591.

also endeavor to connect the Divine spark of our embodied consciousness to the well-being of the planet and the greater human collective. In other words, we must learn to work transpersonally as well as personally. The Sacred Cross can guide us in this pursuit. To work with The Cross in the transpersonal manner inspired by *The Star*, all you need to do is invoke it (using the Long or Short Form) while reorienting its five components away from the personal and toward the collective in the following manner:

- Earth Arm: Unify your consciousness with our connection to the Earth as a human race,

- Heaven Arm: Unify your consciousness with our connection to the sacredness of the human soul and the Divine intelligence,

- Who I Am Arm: Unify your consciousness with our collective imprint as one tribe that lives upon this Earth, "Who We Are" together; and

- What I Know: Unify your consciousness with our human abilities, skills and aptitudes that grant us the ability to positively impact our World, "What We Know" together.

- Heart Center: Co-mingle these transpersonal arms within the Heart of Humanity within you.

When you sit within the heart space central to the transpersonal co-mingling of Earth, Heaven, "Who We Are" and "What We Know," you will be astounded at the insights, inspirations and realizations that come in support of this gesture. Why is this so? It is so because so very few of us are willing and able to focus our awareness toward the transpersonal now…those of us who can and are able, must forge the way for others.

I would like to offer a beautiful image as we complete our discussion of the relationship between The Sacred Cross and *The Star* in the Tarot. As you know, to construct The Sacred Cross we deepen and elevate our consciousness into the spiritual power of the deep Earth and high Heavens, connecting to the Earthlight and the sacred fire of the Divine. As our human heart lives within the spiritual embrace of The Sun, a third source of fire glows from within our Cross. When offered outward with the consciousness of a woman or man of spirit, "Who We Are" and "What We Know" is also filled with the properties of a luminous light. Together the five holy fires of The Sacred Cross create a stunningly beautiful constellation. The five star constellation of The Sacred Cross has the capacity to burn bright in the seen and unseen worlds, in service to ourselves, the greater human and planetary condition and the vast whole of creation.

What better time is there than today to open ourselves to this level of sacred service? The time is swiftly coming for all of us to reach beyond our limited understanding of personal well-being and toward the achievement of our collective well-being. I believe this can only happen when we see ourselves as ambassadors of the human race living in co-creation upon this beautiful planet. The next time you are feeling uncertain what it is you are to be doing with your life, create and sit within The Sacred Cross of the transpersonal; it is here that you will meet the force and form of *The Star*. I promise you that in this contemplation, the list of "requests" will excite, inspire and maybe even, at times, overwhelm you.

I believe that our financial crises, wars and environmental catastrophes are training us like a master trains the young and willful student. Over time we will get the lesson, but for now many of us are wasting time and energy balking at the new directives. Men and women of spirit must poise themselves to be ready and able to make the leap from the personal to the collective. In this pursuit, The Sacred Cross is a very helpful tool.

Concluding Thoughts

With this discussion of the transpersonal application of The Sacred Cross we have completed all that I set out to convey in this book. So it is at this point that I make the following appeal: "Men and women of spirit, do your work!"

Do the work of connecting to the deep Earth, high Heavens, "Who You Are" and "What You Know" on a daily basis. Do the work of mediating spiritual power through you for the benefit of yourself and others. Do the work of relating your sphere to the greater spheres within which you live. Do the work of clarifying and recalibrating yourself to the sacred practices of sleep. Do the work of being an ambassador for humanity to our collective family within the seen and unseen realms of the Earth and Greater Universe.

This may seem like quite a list of "to dos," but you have the tool. The Sacred Cross will assist you with all of these things. Invoke The Sacred Cross for yourself, your soul, a friend, our children, our planet and our collective future potential. In this, may the four-fold grace of Earth, Heaven, "Who You Are" and "What You Know" continually and transformationally embrace you.

ೞ A Note to the Reader ೞ

Twenty-five percent (25%) of the proceeds of *The Sacred Cross: A Transformational Tool for Life* benefit the "Pay it Forward" fund which supports PCA student scholarships. Thank you for your contribution.

Please visit The StarHouse (www.TheStarHouse.org) and Path of the Ceremonials Arts (www.PathoftheCeremonialArts.org) websites for more information about us and the residential and correspondence programs we offer.

Anastacia teaches weekend workshops upon request; please inquire via email at illuminora@yahoo.com.

ೞ Acknowledgements ೞ

I would like to honor and acknowledge my Priestess sister and long time co-creative partner, Lila Sophia Tresemer, without whom this book and its foundations would not be. I would also like to thank the men and women of The Path of the Ceremonial Arts whose presence and prodding keep us striving year by year. Finally, I extend my sincere gratitude to Laine Gerritsen, whose loving heart and sharp eye edited, and thus greatly improved, this manuscript.

❧ About The Author ❧

Anastacia Nutt is a co-founder and facilitator of the *Path of the Ceremonial Arts for Women*, *Path of the Ceremonial Arts for Men* and *Women of Vision* programs associated with The StarHouse and All Seasons Chalice, where she is a Minister.

She is also the author of *Unseen Worlds and Practical Aspects of Spiritual Discernment* (2008) available from RJ Stewart Books. *Unseen Worlds* is a primer for new and advanced practitioners alike. In this book Anastacia relays clear, reputable information as to the promises and pathologies of the unseen worlds. She offers practices that support men and women of spirit in their otherworldly work, creating fertile ground for effective and enduring spiritual and magical relationships.

To find out more about the *Path of the Ceremonial Arts for Women or Men* in the USA or *Women of Vision* in Palestine/Israel, including online and residential courses, visit:

www.PathoftheCeremonialArts.org.

CPSIA information can be obtained
at www.ICGtesting.com
Printed in the USA
BVHW01s0016170118
505335BV00007B/112/P